MIXED ROOTS

A Family History

DAVID ADAMS

Knowing yourself is the beginning of all wisdom - Aristotle

Dedicated to the memory of
my great-grandmother, Sarah Adams

Sarah never did get to see,
The green fields of Ireland,
Nor the flax in full bloom.
But she made sure that her boys did:
And those of us who came after them.

REVIEWS

"I came to know David Adams during the Northern Ireland story of the early to late 1990s; in a time when we began to hope. The story of our "wars" was turning a page, taking us into the beginnings of our "peace". Adams was part of that story and history; an emerging voice from the loyalist community, who would have a seat at the top table when the loyalist ceasefire was announced in 1994, and was part of the negotiations that delivered the political agreement on Good Friday, 1998. He became a columnist and commentator, before joining the Dublin-based international humanitarian organisation, GOAL. He travelled around the world with GOAL in response to numerous natural and manmade disasters. In his humanitarian work, he encountered human suffering on a scale far beyond his Northern Ireland experience. His book, *Mixed Roots*, is another valuable contribution by him to our search for lasting peace. In it he turns to family history - an exploration back in time. What makes us? What is identity? What is important? What is the future?," **Brian Rowan**
Brian Rowan is a former BBC Northern Ireland correspondent, and an author on the peace process

"This book encapsulates the wonder of how our individual and collective history is woven not just through the fabric of this country, but often through threads that stretch across the world - binding events and stories and the direction of life itself. Through painstaking research, and crafted writing, David Adams has delivered a gem. *Mixed Roots* demonstrates that the history of family is happenstance and that we all have the power to choose our own direction." **Máiría Cahill**
Máiría Cahill is an author, columnist, commentator, and survivor

"On the surface, this is a *Who Do You Think You Are?* type story. David Adams has discovered that he is part Indian as a consequence of his paternal great-grandfather, John Adams, soldiering in India. And that John's mixed-race children – the author's grandfather and great-uncle – had to be smuggled to England as illegal immigrants. But this is not just the fascinating story of one man's encounter with his forebears; it is a fully researched account of the unfeeling brutality of colonisation and of army life - specifically how the first impacted on the people's of Ireland and India. Despite owing his existence, as he puts it, to two acts of colonisation, Adams contends that this lies at the root of our ongoing societal divisions in Northern Ireland. *Mixed Roots* isn't just a family story, and it isn't just history; it is a call to deep reflection on how power was abused, and continues to be abused, through class, race, religion, perceived politics… And, most of all, it is a call for a genuine reflection by all of the people of Ireland on how we might move beyond our societal divisions." **Malachi O'Doherty**
Malachi O'Doherty is an author, journalist, and commentator

"In *Mixed Roots*, David Adams tells the story of his paternal ancestors, and, in doing so, casts a highly critical eye over British colonialism, and how it affected the peoples of Ireland and India. There are no happy tales in this book, yet it is hugely uplifting. Seldom in this part of the world is historical narrative untethered from the diktat of community allegiance. David Adams does exactly that. One can only hope that it catches on." **Suzanne Breen**
Suzanne Breen is Political Editor of the Belfast Telegraph

David Adams with President Nelson Mandela

ABOUT THE AUTHOR

From a Northern Irish unionist background, as a (loyalist) politician David Adams helped negotiate the loyalist ceasefire of 1994 and the Good Friday Agreement (GFA) of 1998.

Shortly after the GFA was endorsed at separate referendums in Northern Ireland and the Republic of Ireland, he left politics for good and became a freelance journalist. For more than 10 years, he had a regular column with The Irish Times and scripted and delivered a weekly contributor piece on BBC Radio Ulster's Talkback programme. He also had pieces carried in most major newspapers in Ireland, and made numerous appearances on television and radio programmes.

He later joined the Dublin-based international humanitarian organisation, GOAL, where he spent 13 years or so until his retirement. His time with GOAL took him to all manner of natural and manmade disasters. He worked in, amongst other places, Niger, Uganda, Kenya, Ethiopia, Sudan, South Sudan, Turkey, Syria, Iraq and Sierra Leone.

For his work on the Ebola crisis in Sierra Leone he was awarded a medal by the British government, which was presented at 10 Downing Street by the (then) British Prime Minister David Cameron.

ACKNOWLEDGEMENTS

Many thanks to my brother Nigel, whose perseverance in researching our grandfather, John Henry "Jack" Adams, uncovered the family secret that Jack and his brother, William, had kept for a large part of their lives. His discovery allowed us to gather almost all of the information that led to *Mixed Roots*. And, as though that weren't enough, Nigel also supplied the front-cover illustration for the book. This was taken from a triptych he painted, *Celtic Roots*. I also owe a real debt of gratitude to the author and journalist, Malachi O'Doherty. Malachi was on hand to offer encouragement and advice throughout the process. And process it certainly was. I soon came to learn that the actual writing of a book is the easiest part. Many thanks as well to the author, journalist, and broadcaster Brian Rowan, who, in his quiet way, has done more for peace in Northern Ireland than many of those he has interviewed over the years. Finally, all possible love to my wife Joycelyn, and to our children Kevin, David and Deborah and their families. I would be lost without their unwavering love and support.

NOTE FROM THE AUTHOR

Not only do I outline my family history in *Mixed Roots*, I also describe in detail the times and events my ancestors lived through, and almost invariably offer an opinion on these. Directly expressed opinions are entirely my own. Those expressed through the utterances, thoughts or attitudes of real and invented characters may have been coloured by my own thoughts, but not always. These are, essentially, how I imagine particular people might have responded to particular situations at a given time. The inclusion of fictional characters and their thoughts and conversations was done in order to inject life and rhythm (ie readability) into the book. But the presence of a fictional character seldom, if ever, means that an entire episode is fictional. For instance, the journey from Corfu to India that Private John Adams of the 46th undertook in September 1858 was described in great detail in a diary kept by a travelling companion from the same regiment, Lance Sergeant Samuel Robert Taylor. The dolphin, flying fish, floggings of soldiers, storms at sea, rats in the drinking water, and the donkeys were all mentioned by Taylor. My inventions are John's fellow travellers and their reactions to what they experienced. Similarly, John Adams did of course enlist in the British Army at Newry, County Down in 1855 (taken from his army attestation papers). However, the characters he encountered on the way to Newry, the recruiting Sergeant and others that he met there, and the interactions and dialogue between them are imagined. So, strictly speaking, this is not a history book. But it is far from being a work of fiction, either. All of the major and relatively minor events it covers are matters of indisputable historical fact. Numerous sources are referenced in support of my family history and the descriptions of the times, places, and conditions in which they lived. These include the registration of births, deaths, and marriages; census records; army attestation papers/worldwide indexes/pension and death records; academic studies; contemporary journals and diaries; contemporary newspaper reports; essays by local historians; specialist books; essays by noted authors, and so on.

David Adams

CONTENTS

DEDICATION

ABOUT THE AUTHOR

ACKNOWLEDGEMENTS

NOTE FROM THE AUTHOR

PREFACE 11

PROLOGUE 13
The United Irishmen
John Adams
The Decision

Chapter 1 34
To Newry
Training

Chapter 2 47
Crimea
Attack on Sevastopol
Corfu

Chapter 3 65
To India

Chapter 4 74
India
Karachi
Sarah
Jullundur
Bella

Chapter 5 92
Cawnpore
Lucknow

Chapter 6 106
Chakrata
Peshawar Fever?
Where are the boys?

Chapter 7 126
England
Long Sutton
Eliza Jane
Back to Annahilt

Chapter 8 160
Nanna
Home
Widower

Epilogue 179
John Henry "Jack" Adams
William Adams
Eliza Jane Adams
[Alfred] Henry Pope

List of Illustrations:
Page 6: The author with President Nelson Mandela
Page 13: The symbol of the United Irishmen
Page 33: "At the gate of the workhouse" during Ireland's Great Famine
Page 45: "The Ejectment", an eviction in Ireland
Page 46: The 1855 positions of the Crimean War protagonists
Page 64: Artist's impression of the final battle for Sevastopol
Page 73: Railways supposedly benefitted the Indian people
Page 90: Brigadier-General John Nicholson
Page 91: Great Famine of India
Page 106: All Saints Church, Lucknow, where William and Jack were baptised
Page 121: Peshawar city, circa the 1870s
Page 122: Extracts from John's army attestation papers and pension records
Page 123: Records of Bella's baptism and burial
Page 124: William's and Jack's baptismal records
Page 125: Record of Sarah's death and burial; British census return of 1881 (William and Jack in Somerset)
Page 126: British Army cantonment at Peshawar where Sarah died and was buried
Page 156: British Crimea medal and its Turkish equivalent
Page 157: Records of John's death; Jack's marriage to Lillie Farrell; Lillie's death; and 1901 census showing William living with Eliza Jane and family at Duneight
Page 158: Extracts from William's and Jack's army attestation paper
Page 159: A picture of Jack and Mary on their wedding day; records of their marriage and death
Page 178: "Purtie hokin" as Eliza Jane would have known it

PREFACE

My grandfather, John Henry "Jack" Adams, was always a mysterious character to his grandchildren. He died in 1944, before I was born, but still loomed large over everyone in the extended Adams family. What we were told about him was sparse. According to family legend, Jack had been born and raised in India, the son of a British soldier, and had joined the British army himself as a boy soldier in India, where he served for 12 years. Jack's paternal ancestors supposedly hailed originally from Somerset in England.

A whispered rumour amongst we grandchildren was that my grandmother, Mary, was not Jack's first wife. He had been married before, "to an Indian woman who died in childbirth in India". The child, their first (a daughter) had also died during the birth.

Jack's children, my father and his brothers and sisters, were immensely proud of him, and would grab any excuse to sing his praises. However, they would accept only the most benign questions about him. Anything considered to be in the slightest bit probing would immediately be shut down. "Never look back, always look forward", was a constant Adams family refrain. Our role was to listen about Jack, but not ask questions. This, of course, only served to excite our interest in him. It was clear that something was being hidden. But what?

As they got older, some of the grandchildren tried to research Jack's military history to discover what the "big secret" was, but got nowhere. After a few half-hearted attempts ourselves, scattered over many years, my brother and I decided to give it one final try. Through sheer tenacity and with occasional bits of luck, we finally uncovered the truth.

Jack's story, and that of his older brother, William, went far beyond anything we could ever have imagined. It is one of tragedy and survival, and fear-driven deceptions, some of which were maintained almost until life's end. Essentially, I feel, their personal story is about a search for belonging.

In unearthing my grandfather's history, we couldn't help but uncover that of my great-grandfather, John Adams. John was born at Annahilt, County Down, in the immediate aftermath of the United Irishmen's Rebellion of 1798, and grew up during Ireland's Great Famine. He joined the British Army as a relatively young man and was sent almost immediately to fight at Sevastopol in Crimea. From there he was posted (via Corfu) to India, where he married my great grandmother, Sarah, and their children were born. Thus, *Mixed Roots* became at least as much about John's life and experiences as those of his children.

It would be impossible to chart the lives of my ancestors without describing in detail the social and political conditions of the times they lived through, and how they, along with all other ordinary people, were affected and shaped by them. The backdrop to their lives, both in Ireland and India, was invariably bleak: replete with poverty, famine, disease, religious and political tensions, discrimination, violence, colonialism, and institutional racism.

Colonialism and how it affected native peoples - in this case, those of Ireland and India - lies at the heart of *Mixed Roots*. In any fair-minded consideration of colonialism, its attendant religious and cultural proselytising cannot escape mention. Most specifically, the role this played in attempts by colonisers to destroy and recast native religion(s) and culture(s) in their own nation's image, ostensibly for the benefit of local inhabitants, irrespective of the human misery and long-lasting damage that resulted from it. The people of Ireland hardly need look beyond our shores for evidence of the last.

John Adams was born at a time when it was taken as self-evident that all the people of this island, regardless of differences, did at least have one thing in common, their Irishness. Almost 200 years later, this is no longer the case. Sadly, old enmities born of colonialism persist and hold us fast in a trap of history that has many people native to Ireland denying their Irishness and others defining it solely in their own image. Perhaps an acceptance of what was self-evident in John's time, that we of this island are all equally Irish, would begin to free us from this trap. This, in turn, should allow us together, in all of our thankfully ever-increasing diversity, to begin imagining a future Ireland unencumbered by past hatreds and their resultant horrors. Let us, at the very least, accept that we are one tribe: made up of many different, but all equally Irish, elements.

This is not to suggest a specific *political* solution, but rather, a *societal* one. In liberal democracies, healthy politics will flow naturally from a society at ease with itself. Finally, it is hoped that the story of my ancestors might, in some small way, help challenge the poisonous notions of exceptionalism and purity (whether religious, racial, ethnic, cultural, national, or whatever) that appear, yet again, to be on the march in many parts of the world, threatening the very existence of liberal democratic polities.

David Adams

PROLOGUE

The United Irishmen
In 1791, a small group of Irish Protestants - Theobald Wolfe Tone, Henry Joy McCracken, Thomas Russell, James Napper Tandy, and William Drennan - met in a Belfast tavern to discuss how best they might agitate for political, social and economic reform in Ireland. By the time they parted company, a new organisation had been founded, the Society of United Irishmen, which soon became known simply as the United Irishmen (UI). Contrary to popular belief, the majority of the founders were not Presbyterian but belonged to the Established (ie Anglican) Church of Ireland. Only McCracken and Drennan were Presbyterian.

Ireland at the time was nominally autonomous, but in reality was controlled and supervised by the British government in London. The country, including the local parliament, was dominated by an Anglo-Irish "Protestant Ascendancy" which included the Established Church. All political and financial power, control and prestige rested in the hands of this ascendancy. They owned most of the productive land, taken by conquest by their ancestors, and occupied virtually every seat in the Irish parliament.

In stark contrast, Irish Catholics, who formed the great majority of the population, were forced to bear numerous hardships under Penal Laws. These included, along with much else, being excluded from land ownership and denied voting rights. Irish Presbyterians formed the second largest religious grouping. They, and other non-Anglican Protestants (Dissenters) such as Baptists, Methodists, and Quakers, were permitted to own land and businesses, but were also denied the right to vote. All non-Anglicans were banned from certain professions - such as the law and the judiciary - and had restrictions placed upon the inheriting and bequeathing of land. Catholics could not bear arms or exercise their religion publicly.

Inspired by the American and French revolutions, and not least by Thomas Paine's book, *The Rights of Man*, the stated aims of the founders of the UI were "civil, political and religious liberty for all [the people of Ireland]" and "equal representation…in a national government". This, of course, would entail the full emancipation of Catholics and dissenting Protestants, effectively affording them the same rights as members of the Established Church.

In the same year as the UI was founded, the Roman Catholic Relief Act was passed by the British Parliament. This moved a little way towards relieving some of the burdens that Catholics had long suffered under, but did not come close to the egalitarian emancipation the UI had in mind. The UI grew rapidly in numbers, and soon came to the attention and under the suspicion of the Dublin authorities. When in 1793 war broke out between Britain and France, with whom the UI had long been aligned and from where they sought support, the authorities had the excuse they'd been waiting for. They declared membership of the UI to be illegal, and set about hunting down, arresting and charging anyone they could associate with it.

Whatever faint hopes the UI's founders had of reform under British rule were dashed. They decided the time had come to, in the words of Wolfe Tone, "substitute the common name of Irishman for Protestant, Catholic and Dissenter" and "break the connection with England, the never failing source of all our political evils". As this could only mean driving the forces of the British Crown out of Ireland, they began gathering and storing weapons and organising themselves along military lines.

For their part, the authorities were relentless in their attempts at suppression. Nor were they overly fussy about adhering to legal niceties.

ANNAHILT AND THE '98 RISING

Now woe be on thee, Annahilt,
And woe be on the day,
When brother, lover, both were slain,
And with them, Betsy Gray.
(Poem, unattributed)

Located in the northern part of County Down, the tiny village and civil parish of Annahilt sits roughly halfway between Hillsborough village and Ballynahinch town, about four miles from each, and just over seven miles to the south of the much larger town of Lisburn.

Annahilt's population was a mere 1,148 in the 2001 census. It was home to even fewer people in 1830, when my great-grandfather, John Adams, was born there. As late as 1868, the village consisted of only a schoolhouse, a church and a few dwellings scattered about a crossroads. *(1)*

At first glance, then, Annahilt would seem a rather inconsequential place. But closer inspection shows it to have been close witness to quite a few historic events in the lead up to and immediate aftermath of the United Irishmen rebellion of 1798. Indeed, two of its residents were participants in a terrible atrocity that ensured their names would go down in infamy.

William Orr

Write his merits on your mind,
Morals pure and manners kind,
In his head, as on a hill,
Virtue placed her citadel.
Why cut off in palmy youth?
Truth he spoke and acted truth,
Countrymen unite, he cried
And died - for what his Saviour died.

(From *"The Wake of William Orr"* by William Drennan,
a founding member of the United Irishmen.)

William Orr was a young Presbyterian farmer of Farranshane near Antrim town. He had submitted a number of articles to the Northern Star, a Belfast newspaper openly sympathetic to the United Irishmen's cause, and these had brought him to the attention of the authorities. He was alerted to his imminent arrest by a Presbyterian minister, himself a member of the United Irishmen, and went into hiding for a time. Orr was apprehended, however, when he visited the home of his dying father, which had been kept under watch by the British. He was accused of administering the United Irishmen oath to two British soldiers of the Fifeshire Fencibles and sent for trial, to be held in September, 1797.

It was clear from the outset of the trial that the soldiers were lying. When cross-examined they would contradict one another and, on occasion, each would even contradict previous statements he himself had made. Despite the jury being handpicked by the authorities, the evidence was so flimsy and tainted that after being locked away for more than 11 hours of overnight deliberations, its members returned to the courtroom and announced that they were unable to reach a verdict. They were sent away to deliberate further. But not before the elderly jury foreman, Archibald Thompson, was put under heavy pressure to only return with "the right verdict". The jury duly found Orr guilty, but with a recommendation for mercy. This was all the authorities needed. After government representatives in Dublin had been consulted, the recommendation of the jury was ignored, and two days later William Orr was sentenced to hang. Despite Archibald Thompson making public the threats that he had received, other jurors outlining inducements such as bottles of whiskey being passed to them while they were deliberating, and a juror telling how he was assured that if he changed his verdict to guilty Orr would be treated leniently, the verdict and sentence were allowed stand. One of the soldiers even admitted to a Presbyterian minister that he had lied about Orr administering the oath. But it made no difference. William Orr (31) was publicly hanged at 2:45pm on October 14, 1797 at common ground on the outskirts of Carrickfergus.

A large crowd, including most of the townspeople of Carrickfergus, was in attendance to "express disgust at this act of shameful injustice". Orr met his fate in a manner befitting the hero he was about to become. Just before he mounted the scaffold, he reached out and handed his hat as a keepsake and act of friendship to a Catholic tenant of his who was standing nearby, openly weeping. As the hangman's noose was placed around his neck, Orr declared, "I am no traitor. I die for a persecuted country. Great Jehovah receive my soul. I die in the true faith of a Presbyterian." William Orr's body was buried in his sister's grave at Templepatrick. His name was not inscribed on the headstone. It was only in 1997, the bicentenary of his death, that a plaque bearing his name was mounted at the grave.

Orr was a proud United Irishman, as he made clear in a tract bearing his last words that was widely distributed after his death. But he denounced how his trail had been conducted, and made clear his innocence of the charges that had been laid against him.

If Orr's hanging and other similar acts by the authorities were intended to deter people from joining the ranks of the United Irishmen, they had the opposite effect. Far from being cowed, the country was outraged. During 1797, membership of the United Irishmen swelled to an estimated 200,000.

William and Owen McKenna, Peter Carron, and Daniel Gillan

In coffins they were hurried,
From Blaris Moor were carried,
And hastily were buried,
As thousands sank in grief,

They cried, "Grania! we much wonder,
You rise not from your slumber,
With a voice as loud as thunder,
To give us some relief."

Extract from, *"Blaris Moor"*, a song written in 1797

Earlier in the same year that Orr was hanged, 1797, the execution of four young United Irishmen had taken place. The location this time was only a few miles from Annahilt, at Blaris Moor. Since at least the early 1700s, the flat, sandy fields of the civil parish of Blaris [*where this author was born and grew up*], just off the main road between Lisburn and Hillsborough, had been home to a military encampment, Blaris Moor. Stationed there in 1797, along with other regiments, was a detachment of the Monaghan Militia. Early in April a senior officer of the militia, Col Charles Leslie, was greatly disturbed to learn that Presbyterian radicals from Belfast had persuaded a number of his men to swear allegiance to the United Irishmen. The Belfast people had for some time been travelling out to Blaris at weekends, ostensibly to furnish the soldiers with tobacco, small items of clothing and other sundries.

Leslie assembled his men and promised to seek a pardon from the Lord Lieutenant for those who admitted their involvement in the conspiracy. To his astonishment and horror, more than 70 soldiers stepped forward and confessed to taking the United Irishmen's oath. Not surprisingly, it was generally agreed by the military authorities that they could hardly execute 70-odd men. But an example had to made. So, after a time all were pardoned except four, who, it was claimed, had sworn the others in and were deemed to be the ring-leaders.

The four, Peter Carron, Daniel Gillan, and brothers William and Owen McKenna, were taken to Belfast, tried by court martial and found guilty of "exciting, causing, and joining in, a Mutiny and Sedition" in the Monaghan Militia. They were sentenced to be shot at Blaris Moor. On the day of the execution, the Monaghan Militia and various other units slow marched from Belfast to Blaris escorting two carts carrying the prisoners, their clergy and their coffins. Crowds lined the 10-mile route, sometimes sombre and at other times angry and openly hostile to the army officers; men shouted words of support and encouragement to the four young men, while women openly wept. At precisely 1 p.m. on May 17, 1797, the four young men were ordered to kneel on their coffins at Blaris Moor and were shot to death by firing squad. After the execution, as a warning to others, the assembled troops were marched slowly past the bodies as they lay on the ground. The bodies were then taken to just within the gateway of Blaris Old Cemetery and buried in an unmarked grave. The father of the McKenna brothers, Owen Snr, had travelled from his home in Monaghan to witness the trial and subsequent execution of his sons. When asked why they and their two colleagues had refused to name the people from Belfast who had inducted them into the United Irishmen, he is reputed to have said, "I can bear to see my sons die, but not for them to live [as] traitors and slaves in the land of their birth."

The McKee Family

And they set fire to the dwelling,
And in the inferno Hugh lost his life,
As did his five sons and three daughters,
And also his Bridesmaid wife.

From a poem, *"The Curse of a Bride Jilted"*, (unattributed)

On occasion, the United Irishmen could be every bit as brutal as their oppressors.

About eight miles from Annahilt, and a mile short of Saintfield, lived a large family by the name of McKee. The father, Hugh McKee, was a relatively prosperous farmer who grew flax and spun yarn.

It was said that on his wedding day, McKee's intended bride was lengthily detained on her way to the (civil) ceremony. Exasperated, he turned to a waiting bridesmaid and asked if she would "wed him instead". The bridesmaid readily agreed. The intended bride turned up just as the marriage ceremony ended, and was said to be so angered that she put a curse on the newly-weds.

McKee's success as a farmer was reflected in the large house he shared with his wife and grown-up children, five sons and three daughters. A blind girl of 13, a relative of the family, and a male servant, John Boles, also lived with the McKees. The family was deeply unpopular in the area. They were widely known as ultra-royalists who would bait and bully United Irishmen at every opportunity, and were considered even by other loyalists to be decidedly obnoxious people.

Members of the family would challenge and sometimes fire shots at people passing-by their house at night, to the extent that locals began to make a detour through nearby fields to avoid coming close to the McKee property.

One night a certain Samuel Adams, a leading member of the United Irishmen in the Saintfield area, decided to continue walking on the road rather than take to the fields. When he came close to the McKee property he was promptly shot through the arm and side by Nelly McKee, one of Hugh's daughters. She then grabbed a hatchet and made to finish Adams off, on the unarguable basis that "dead men tell no tales". Two Scottish soldiers who were at the McKee house to protect the family took the hatchet from Nellie and effectively saved Adams' life.

It is possible, likely even, that Samuel Adams' presence in the vicinity of the McKee home was anything but innocent. When attempts had been made to raise a royalist corps of yeomanry in the Saintfield area, it was widely known that the McKees were the only people who expressed a willingness to join. The family subsequently became concerned for their safety and applied to the authorities for protection. Hence the Scottish soldiers who, fortunately for Adams, were in the house when the shooting took place. It is more than feasible that Adams was in fact there to either plan or lead an attack upon the McKees. Whatever the true story, Nellie McKee effectively sealed her family's fate that night - and helped bring to fruition the "Curse of the Jilted Bride".

On Saturday, June 9, 1798 a large contingent of Saintfield United Irishmen, on their way to do battle with British forces at Ballynahinch, decided to make a detour to the McKee's house. They were seeking revenge for the attack on Adams, and to take possession of a large stockpile of weapons and ammunition that the authorities gave to McKee when they had to withdraw their military protection. Hugh McKee, having been alerted that morning to a large, well-armed crowd on its way to his house, had time with his family to barricade themselves in.

The United Irishmen arrived shortly after noon and demanded that McKee and his sons hand over their munitions and join them on the march to Ballynahinch. When McKee refused they attacked the house, but it was so well barricaded and they couldn't gain entry. A standoff ensued, with periodic gunfire being exchanged between the house and the attackers and no sign of the situation being resolved one way or the other. Eventually a ladder was fetched, and a United Irishman climbed on to the roof of the house. He broke through the roof and tossed a clump of burning straw on to a large pile of flax in the attic below. The flax immediately burst into flames and within minutes the house was ablaze.

The McKee family huddled together, still refusing to leave their home. And that was how 11 bodies were found by the authorities: clinging together, almost reduced to ash. John Boles, the servant, had jumped through a window and made a run for it. But he had hardly taken a few steps outside before he was run through with a pike, mortally wounded and left for dead. He died two days later, but not before he had given the names of some of the attackers to a neighbour who came to his aid after the United Irishmen had left.

Upon their arrests, two of those named as perpetrators turned Kings Evidence, and were awarded pensions for life. On their testimony and what Boles had told the neighbour, 11 men were tried, found guilty, and hanged for their part in the killing of the McKees. Of the 11, it was claimed locally that 10 were in fact innocent, with only the leader of the attack, John Breeze, guilty as charged.

Henry Munro

Tell my country I have deserved better of her.

Henry Munro, speaking on the gallows at Lisburn on June 17, 1798

Henry Munro was a native of Lisburn, a large town that straddles the counties of Down and Antrim, and sits six or so miles to the north of Annahilt. Born in 1758 to a Presbyterian tradesman of Scottish descent, Munro was raised as an Anglican. From childhood he worshipped with his father, mother and two sisters at Lisburn (Church of Ireland) Cathedral. After leaving school, he went into the trade for which Lisburn was then famous, linen. After a lengthy apprenticeship he struck out on his own and became a successful and, by all accounts very honourable, merchant.

After witnessing the public flogging of a friend named Hood in his home town, Munro was said to have taken strong umbrage against the authorities. He resented their abuses of power and their treatment of ordinary citizens, particularly Catholics.

He joined the United Irishmen in 1795 and was soon elected to its County Antrim executive committee. In 1798, a Presbyterian minister and senior member of the United Irishmen in Down, the Reverend William Steel Dickson, agreed to accept the position of Adjutant-General of the United Irish forces in the county after the previous occupant, Thomas Russell, had been arrested. Only a few days before the planned Rising, however, Dickson himself was arrested. Henry

Munro was asked to take Dickson's place and, despite him having no military experience, he felt it his solemn duty to accept.

On Monday June 11, Munro marched with his main force from Creevy Rocks outside Saintfield to Ednavady Hill near Ballynahinch. Those under his command numbered approximately 7,000. They had been joined by a large number of North Down United Irishmen, still jubilant at having ambushed and defeated a contingent of British soldiers at the Battle of Saintfield the previous Saturday.

On his approach to Ballynahinch to engage the insurgents, the British commander, General Nugent, had ordered that the towns of Killinchy, Killyleagh, Saintfield, and all cottages and farms along the way should be burned. The smoke and flames alerted Munro to their approach. He sent a force of 500 men to occupy a position at Windmill Hill, Ballynahinch, in an attempt to halt Nugent's progress. But the British manoeuvred to take up a position between the town and the hill, and opened fire with cannon. The ensuing battle between the opposing sides raged from 6:00pm to 9-00pm, until eventually Munro's troops were forced to abandon Windmill Hill.

Ballynahinch was in flames. Later that evening hordes of drunken soldiers could be seen roaming its streets celebrating their victory. Munro's senior commanders suggested that this would be a perfect time to mount a surprise attack and take the town. Munro demurred, saying that to do so would be taking "ungenerous advantage". He was, it would appear, as honourable as ever - on this occasion, to a fault. When word spread of his decision, many of his men deserted, and still more left during the night.

The following morning, Wednesday the 13th, battle resumed, this time much of it at close quarters, and lasted throughout the day. Men, and a few women, fought one another with pike, sword, knife and musket, and whatever else came to hand, until, at 7-00pm, Munro's exhausted troops retreated in disorder and began to disperse. The Battle of Ballynahinch had been lost. It was estimated that more than 400 United Irishmen and around 50 British troops had been killed, with hundreds more, on either side, wounded.

Nor was the killing over. As Munro's people tried to escape and make their way home, British troops set off in hot pursuit. Scores of innocent civilians were killed or wounded by rampaging soldiers eager to take their anger out on any Irish person they encountered. Munro escaped the field of battle, and began to make his way back to Lisburn. But outside Dromore he was betrayed by a farmer, Billy Holmes, who promised to hide him for £5 and a shirt. As soon as he was hidden, Holmes informed the Hillsborough yeomanry and Munro was arrested.

He was marched from Dromore to Lisburn and held in a temporary prison at Castle Street in the town. His friends rallied round him. A Reverend Cupples, who lived on Castle Street, had Munro's meals sent to him, and a Mr. George Whitla delivered him a full suit of new clothes. On Monday June 17, he was tried by court-martial, quickly found guilty and sentenced to hang, with the sentence to be carried out immediately. Munro asked to meet with his church minister in order to receive his last Holy Communion. His request was granted. He was then marched, with hands bound, along Castle Street to Market Square, where a gallows had been erected in full view of his house.

As Munro made to climb the ladder to the gallows, the bottom rung gave way and he fell against a guard. But he soon righted himself, regained his composure and climbed on to the gallows platform. As the hangman placed the noose around his neck, Munro looked to the assembled crowd and spoke his last words, "Tell my country I have deserved better of her."

As he fell to his death, opposite his home and in full view of his family, a loud wailing erupted from the crowd. But the authorities had not finished with Henry Munro just yet. His body was taken down and decapitated, and the head mounted on a pike at one corner of Market Square. Another three United Irishmen were hanged in Lisburn that day, Richard Vincent, George Crabbe, and Thomas Armstrong. Their severed heads were placed at the other three corners of the square. Henry Munro's remains were buried in the family plot at Lisburn Cathedral.

Elizabeth "Betsy" Gray

The star of evening slowly rose,
Through shades of twilight gleaming,
It shone to witness Erin's woes,
Her children's life-blood streaming:
'Twas then, sweet star, thy pensive ray,
Fell on the cold unconscious clay,
That wraps the breast of Bessie Gray,
In softened lustre beaming

Extract from, *"Nancy of the Branching Tresses",* a poem by Mary Balfour

Elizabeth "Betsy" Gray was one of a small number of women who fought alongside the United Irishmen at the Battle of Ballynahinch on June 12-13, 1798. The daughter of Hans Gray, a widowed Presbyterian farmer from Gransha near Comber, Betsy was 21-years-old when she went to Ballynahinch in the company of her brother George Gray and her fiancé William "Willie" Boal. According to those who knew her, she was an attractive young woman of average female height and slight of build. Some accounts have it that she went into battle astride a white horse and carrying the United Irishmen banner.

Whatever about a white horse, eye-witnesses from both sides of the conflict were agreed that Betsy fought as well as any man. Upon suffering defeat at Ballynahinch, the United Irishmen retreated in chaos with the forces of the Crown in hot pursuit. Despite their commander, Major-General George Nugent, urging his men to "…be merciful" the victorious army sacked Ballynahinch, yet again, burning 63 houses to the ground, while British cavalry and local militiamen scoured the countryside, raiding homes and killing indiscriminately. One of those who escaped the field of battle and made it home safely to Ballyroney near Banbridge was a man named William Brunty. He was a younger brother of the Reverend Patrick Brontë, who would become father to Charlotte, Emily, and Anne Brontë of worldwide literary fame. It was said that Patrick changed his surname back to its original Huguenot derivation in order to distance himself from his brother (who at the time was on the run for his involvement in the United Irishmen and with whose politics he vehemently disagreed). Betsy Gray, with her two companions, also escaped the Battle of Ballynahinch. Betsy's name, too, would be immortalised, but for entirely different reasons to the Brontës.

In making their escape from Ballynahinch, her young male companions decided it would be safer for Betsy if she went slightly ahead of them. As a woman travelling alone, they surmised, she would arouse less suspicion. However, at Ballycreen, about 2 miles equidistant from Hillsborough and Annahilt, she was detained by a detachment of soldiers from the Hillsborough Yeomanry. Seeing this, George and Willie ran to help her and were immediately gunned down. When Betsy tried to go to the aid of her brother and fiancé, stretching out an arm in a vain attempt to reach them, a cavalryman named Jack Gill slashed at her with a sabre, cutting off her extended hand. Then yeomen Thomas Nelson and James Little both shot her in the head. The yeomen left the young trio lying where they fell. But not before Little had desecrated Betsy's body, removing items of her clothing and some meagre jewellery.

The following day, Matthew Armstrong, the young son of a local farmer, found the three mutilated bodies. He and two neighbours carried them to his family's land and buried them in a single grave. As word spread of the atrocity, the country was once again outraged. Not least the people of Annahilt who soon learned of the involvement of two their neighbours.

It is likely that Nelson and Little would have known Betsy and George Gray, and possibly Willie Boal, as Annahilt was less than 10 miles from the Gray's family home at Gransha. It is beyond doubt that many other residents of Annahilt would indeed have known them, and sympathised with their cause. Local tensions were further exacerbated when, a few days after the killings, Little's wife was seen to be wearing Betsy's earrings and petticoat.

Little and Nelson and their families were ostracised by all who knew them. Abuse was shouted at them as they passed by and their children were often stoned on their way to and from school. Nelson soon moved out of Annahilt, but Little and his family remained. Local animosity towards descendants of the Little family lasted well into the twentieth century. It is said that successive generations of worshippers at Annahilt's Church of Ireland church would refuse to share a pew with them.

Given the fate of the McKee family, the Littles probably owed their lives to being on the winning side in 1798. At Annahilt, as with everywhere else, surviving United Irishmen and their sympathisers would for a long time be ultra-careful not to bring themselves to the attention of the authorities. Still, each year locals would visit the grave of Betsy and her brother and fiancé and lay flowers in their memory. In 1890, after a proposal by the Henry Joy McCracken Memorial Literary Society in Belfast, a formal stone and surround was mounted there, paid for by James Gray, a grand-nephew of Betsy and George.

After the 1800 Acts of Union, Presbyterians and other non-conformist Protestants transferred their loyalty to the parliament at Westminster. Consequently, they resisted the Catholic-supported Home Rule Bill of 1886, which would have transferred legislative independence to an Irish government in Dublin. Tensions around home rule were still running high when in 1898 nationalist ceremonies were planned all over Ireland to mark the centenary of the rising of the United Irishmen. One such ceremony was to be held at the graveside of Betsy Gray. But the night before it was due to take place, loyalists smashed the headstone to pieces with sledgehammers and uprooted and scattered the metal surround. The next day, when parties of Catholic nationalists arrived from Belfast, they were attacked and driven away by a crowd of locals. The religious sectarianism that Betsy Gray, George Gray, and Willie Boal had despised, fought against, and given their lives to oppose had, quite literally, danced on their grave.

The charge has often been laid that Britain, in a classic example of the divide-and-rule tactic at which it was a master, managed to buy-off Irish non-conformist Protestants by affording them political and religious liberties while withholding the same from Irish Catholics. And there is truth to that. However, a number of sectarian attacks on minority Protestant communities in the south of Ireland in the wake of the failed 1798 Rising may have made the "buying-off" an awful lot easier than might otherwise have been the case.

Most notable amongst these attacks occurred at Scullabogue in County Wexford on June 05, 1798 when up to 200 Protestant men, women, and children (depending on who you choose to believe) from in and around the area were rounded up and locked inside a barn, which was then set on fire killing everyone inside. People trying to escape the barn were shot, stabbed and beaten to death or forced back into the flames. Upon hearing of Scullabogue, Irish Protestants of all shades might just have wondered if their future would be more secure with Britain, after all. *(2)*

John Adams

Nothing is known for certain of John Adams' parents, or whether he had any siblings. There is reason to suspect that his father may have been named William, and was very likely a weaver (the trade that John himself would adopt). But no conclusive evidence exists.

As something of a grisly aside, grave robbing had become a feature of Irish life (or, more accurately, Irish death) around the time of John's birth, with at least a few recorded instances very close to his birthplace. In September 1831, two medical students living at Dromara, County Down, were arrested for trying to export two stolen bodies to Scotland. One of the bodies was of a man from Ballynahinch and the other of a woman from Dromara. Both were reclaimed by relatives. The previous year, in December 1830, the sexton at Lambeg church just outside Lisburn was dismissed from his post because he "must have had knowledge of the disinterment of bodies".

Most of the Irish bodies were being shipped to Scotland for medical research at the Edinburgh anatomy school of Robert Knox. Knox's was not the only anatomy school in Scotland, but it must surely have been amongst the most voracious. During 1828 alone, it made use of more than 400 bodies. Such was the appetite for corpses at the school, two Irishmen living in the city, William Burke and William Hare, decided to circumvent the process by murdering people. Why go to the bother of robbing graves when you can simply kill people for their bodies?

Before they were caught in November 1828, Burke and Hare had sold 17 corpses to Robert Knox - 16 of which were of people they had suffocated to death. The capture of Burke and Hare, and the ensuing scandal, led to increased measures to prevent grave robbing in Edinburgh. This in turn led to Knox having to import greater numbers of bodies from Ireland. As an indicator of the contempt in which Irish people of all religions and politics were held in Britain at the time, the following was proposed as a possible solution to grave robbing by a London newspaper in the spring of 1828: *"Let the body of every Irish pauper who comes to this country uninvited, and dies here, be given to the anatomical schools. The plan would relieve us in a great measure from the influx of Paddies, as they would much rather deposit their bodies at home, than give at all events, a few additional subjects to our anatomists."* (Anon 1828). This proposal can hardly be put down to a gut reaction to the murderous activities of Irishmen Burke and Hare. It would be many months before those two were apprehended. It isn't hard to imagine what Irish people might have thought of this extract, coming as it did from an English newspaper: *"...who comes to this country uninvited..."*. *(3)*

Thirty-two years separated the rebellion of 1798 and the birth of John Adams at Annahilt, and in the intervening period the community into which he was born had switched their political allegiance. However, 32 years amounts to little more than the blink of an eye in Irish historical terms. Aspects of history may be celebrated or reviled in Ireland; events are often exaggerated, diminished, revised or conveniently ignored, but they are seldom forgotten. Where there is forgetfulness, it is by design and takes generations to fully achieve. *(4)*

John would have grown up in the shadow of the '98 rebellion, listening to the stories of all that had happened in the immediate surrounds of Annahilt and in nearby towns and villages. He would have heard the story of Betsy Gray, and learned why the Littles were outcasts within his community. Her grave was, at most, two miles from the family home. Was his family amongst those who laid flowers every year in memory of Betsy?

Little and Dawson are proof that there were indeed loyalists living at Annahilt during the '98 Rising. But local reaction to the killing of Betsy and her brother and fiancé, and the fact that animosity towards two of the perpetrators lasted for generations, strongly suggests there were an awful lot more sympathisers to the cause of the United Irishmen living there. Records appear to show there was no Adams family living at Annahilt before 1829. So John's antecedents obviously moved there from somewhere else.

There had always been a number of Adams families, all weavers, living in and around Saintfield, only eight miles north of Annahilt. It seems likely, therefore, that it was from Saintfield John's family came. If so, were they related to the Samuel Adams of the United Irishmen who had been shot in the arm and stomach by Nellie McKee? There is no way of telling, but it's certainly possible.

A terrible tragedy that John Adams did have direct experience of was the Great Famine (1845-1851) when a failure for successive years of the potato crop in Ireland (allied to the almost total abandonment of the Irish people to their fate by the British government) led to a prolonged period of mass starvation and disease across the island. Out of a population of six million, the Great Famine eventually claimed one million lives and forced another two million to emigrate. Ireland's misery was compounded by the heartlessness of many of its landlords, both large and small. Between 1845 and 1854 more than quarter-of-a-million labourers and tenant farmers were evicted from their homes. They and their families were simply turned out and left to fend for themselves. For many, an eviction amounted to being sentenced to a slow, tortuous death.

Although the people of John's native County Down did not suffer nearly as badly as those in other parts of Ireland, they did not escape the famine unscathed. Far from it. Flax may have been the predominant crop in Down, as it was across much of the rest of Ulster, but it was far from the only one. There were Co Down families who, like their fellow countrymen and -women, relied almost entirely upon the potato for survival.

At the height of the famine up to 30 per cent of the people in rural parts of Down, such as at Annahilt where John lived, were wholly reliant on relief aid. Not all landlords were heartless, of course. A landowning family, the Andrews of Comber, 16 miles from Annahilt, did their best to help local people by importing a large quantity of Indian corn and buckwheat peas from France as a contribution to the relief aid. But when cooked the corn and peas proved inedible to even, more likely *especially*, the starving people, and had to be fed to livestock. By January 1847, according to the *Down Recorder* newspaper, in the village of Crossgar, some 11 miles from Annahilt, there were,

"...about 240 persons in this village in an utterly destitute state and if something is not done for them the consequences will be frightful. The people, we are assured, are literally starving. Is not this a melancholy state of things within five miles of the town of Downpatrick?"

During his teenage years, John would doubtless have witnessed at first-hand the deadly effects on friends and neighbours, and possibly even family members, of the starvation and its related diseases, such as dysentry and scurvy. At Loughaghery Presbyterian Church, in his own parish of Annahilt, baptisms plummeted during the famine on account of parishioners dying or emigrating, and the numbers never fully recovered. John would surely have encountered some of the many thousands of families that were roaming far and wide across the Irish countryside in search of food. And no doubt would occasionally have come upon the body of a loved one of theirs whose search had ended in a ditch or by a roadside. Nor were the workhouses of much help. Those who made it to a workhouse may have received a tiny amount of food but conditions were abominable, making it debatable whether the chances of survival there were any better than scrabbling for sustenance outside.

The general policy of workhouses was to make them as unappealing as possible, and this they managed to do. The poor were crowded in on top of one another, resulting in sickness and fever spreading like wildfire amongst them. Deaths in the Belfast workhouse rose from an average of 300 per year to 1,500 in 1847.

In March of 1847, the matron of Downpatrick workhouse, a Miss McCreedy, died from the effects of a fever she contracted in the course of her duties. The *Down Recorder* noted, *"We had the pleasure of knowing Miss McCreedy since she became matron and from the excellent state of discipline in which she had the establishment, we can truly say that her loss there will be severely felt."* It is telling that the newspaper should consider her most noteworthy accomplishment was to instill an *"excellent state of discipline"* in the workhouse.

It could hardly have come as a surprise that Miss McCreedy contracted a fever. A month earlier, a committee set up to inquire into the state of the Downpatrick workhouse's fever hospital reported: *"There are at present under treatment about double the number of patients that the building was originally calculated to accommodate. The store room has been emptied of its contents and converted into a ward but a great number of patients have to lie upon the floor, in the spaces between the beds. And what is still worse, in many cases two patients [are] in one bed. We have a daily influx of patients and from the present condition of the poorer classes and the prospect yet before them, we have every reason to dread a continued increase in still greater proportion."*

Census records show that County Down's population declined by 44,000 between 1841 and 1851. Ireland's population had been exploding prior to 1845, so such a dramatic decline during this period could only have been a direct result of people dying or emigrating to escape from the Great Famine. *(5)*

John Adams may have encountered cholera, another by-product of the famine, which swept through many of the most weakened and starving populations on the island. If not, it was merely the deferment of a meeting between himself and this deadly disease. For a decision he made in the spring of 1855 determined that he and cholera would run headlong into one another later in his life, when it would wreak havoc upon him and his immediate family. But that still lay many years ahead.

The Decision

Early in 1855 John Adams finally came to a decision. Or rather, it came to him. For it was John's way to mull a thorny issue over for a few days, and if he could not decide on the best way to proceed, push it to the back of his mind and think no more about it. He would simply go about his business and wait for a decision to arrive, unforced, to him. Once this happened, as it invariably did, there would be no changing his mind. Or, as those who knew him best would put it, "there'd be no turning him". The same people would have described John as a decent sort, who "if he can't do you a good turn, he won't do you a bad one, either". He didn't fall out with people easily but if someone got on the wrong side of him he didn't forgive easily either. He tended to be "a bit deep" but "with no back doors in him". It was this hard-to-read aspect of him that came immediately to the minds of those whom he shared his decision with. They hadn't seen it coming, but that did not surprise them. Neither was there any point in asking him if he was sure. Of course he was! John wasn't looking for advice or reassurance, but was simply letting them know what he intended to do. All that was left for his nearest and dearest to do was to shake his hand, tell him that he'd be sorely missed, and wish him the very best of luck.

Perhaps it was the recent extremes of weather in his native land that had prompted John's decision. To describe the previous year, 1854, as exceptionally dry would be a gross understatement. Almost a century later it still ranked among the five driest years in Ireland's history. Flax, upon which John's livelihood as a weaver depended, had suffered badly from the drought. A hardy little plant, flax has been known to survive in some of the toughest climatic conditions around the world. But it struggled to cling to life in the hard-baked Irish soil of 1854. The dry spell came almost immediately in the wake of the Great Famine, when the potato crop was all but wiped out by disease. His experience of the consequences of the sudden failure of the staple crop, and almost exclusive source of food and means of income for the majority of the people on the island, may have led John to worry about the vulnerability of his own sole means of income. After the year that had just passed, he might have feared that flax could easily go the same way as the potato. Could he afford to gamble on that not happening?

Just as 1854 was to go down on record as one of the driest-ever years in Ireland, the winter that followed was not to be outdone. It is recorded as one of the coldest. For decades afterwards, the winter of 1854-1855 was referred to in Ireland as the winter of "The Great Frost". Often accompanied by heavy falls of snow, a deep frost persisted through late 1854 and well into the following year. Indeed, 1855 delivered the third-coldest February of all time. And, as though not enough soul-sapping records had already been broken, the first five months of 1855 are still on record as Ireland's coldest ever Spring. *(6)*. Aside from the weather and what it might portend, John surely had other reasons to consider his position in life. Weaving was a dirty, backbreaking, mind-numbing occupation. The busiest time came after the flax had been pulled in late August, and lasted throughout the winter. A weaver would spend his winter days and nights bent over a loom in a dank, often smoke-filled, barely-heated stone-built cottage. From early evening onwards, as he worked the rough flax through his machine by hand, he would have only light from the fireplace and a candle as a guide.

Even during the mildest of winters weaving was a freezing, tortuous occupation. How much more so must it have been during the winter of 1854-1855? It was not as if he was being well compensated for his efforts, either. Depending on the quality of linen he was able to produce (coarse, medium, or superfine) he could earn somewhere between 5s - 3d and 17s - 6d per week. And this only if he worked 15-hour days, seven days a week. In raw spending power, these sums equate to someone in 2021 having to work 105 hours a week to earn between £35:50 and £110:50. *(7)*

Given the toll taken on flax by the drought of the previous year, its subsequent scarcity, and the impossibility of being able to weave medium or superfine linen from the undersized plants that had managed to survive, it is certain that during the winter of 1884-1885 John would have thought himself lucky if he was able to earn anywhere close to 5s - 3d per week.

Perhaps rather than worrying about the future of his livelihood, John had decided that he wanted to escape it altogether. He was a single man who didn't rent or own any land, so he lived with and worked alongside his family. In effect, he was employed by them. On the face of it then, there were no strong ties to his job and home place . But only on the face of it. There was indeed something - or, more accurately, someone - that might well have acted as an accelerant to the decision that he made. At 25-years John Adams was a young man, but only if viewed through a modern lens. In the Ireland of the mid-1880s the average life expectancy of a man was around 40 years. So, in relative terms, he had in fact reached slightly beyond middle-age. In a few short years he would have no other option but to stick with the weaving.

To even reach 40 years in the mid-1880s was in large part down to good fortune. Poor diet, insanitary living conditions, and unhealthy and dangerous working environments meant that one had not only to avoid suffering a serious accident, but manage to escape the innumerable potentially fatal diseases that were prevalent at the time. Many of these diseases and their causes had yet to be identified, never mind cures or inoculations against them developed. This was a time long before anything even approaching government or societal safety-nets such as free medical care, unemployment benefit, welfare support and the like were in place.

It was a simple fact of life that if you became seriously ill and, like the overwhelming majority of people, couldn't afford a doctor, there was every likelihood you would die. If you lost your home or job, or became unemployable for any reason, it was a similar story. Without the support of family and friends, who themselves were struggling to survive, you might easily starve to death. The everyday enemies of ordinary Irish people of all religions at the time were abject poverty, susceptibility to illness and disease, and a life-threatening reliance on the whims of landlords and employers. As it has been succinctly put: "The gap between living and dying, even in a good year, was perilously narrow."*(8)* There was always the workhouse to fall back on, of course. But these were virtually non-existent outside of Ireland's cities and large towns. Besides which, for the reasons noted above, even the destitute tended to stay as far away from those establishments as possible. Ireland's workhouses did little to improve their reputation during the Great Famine, and a great deal that tarnished it. It was universally felt that when someone went into the workhouse they tended not to come out again. At least not under their own steam. It was against this background that John Adams decided to leave everything behind and take a job with long term security. One that, along with a decent steady wage, came with free medical care, an education if he desired it, and a pension at the end of it. In the late spring of 1855, he decided to join the British army. There was a chance, of course, that John might be killed in some far-off conflict. But the risks weren't much greater than they were of him dying of overwork, disease, or starvation at home. Besides, if he were to perish in some foreign land, at least he would die with the sun on his face, far removed from the bitter bite of the Great Frost. John's decision would have far-reaching implications for himself and many of those who came after him.

1) Griffiths Valuations; Tithe Applotment Books 1847 - 1864, https://www.askaboutireland.ie/griffith-valuation/
2) The Summer Soldiers, by A.T.Q. Stewart, The Blackstaff Press, 1995; Betsy Gray, or, the Hearts of Down, by W.G. Lyttle, 1896; The Monaghan Militia & the Tragedy of Blaris Moor, by Brian MacDonald, The Clogher Record, vol. 16, no. 2, Clogher Historical Society, 1998, pp. 123–43, https://doi.org/10.2307/20641353; Recollections of the Battle of Ballynahinch. The Belfast Magazine and Literary Journal,(1825) 1(1), 56–64. https://doi.org/10.2307/20495499; Memories of '98, by WS Smith, Ulster Journal of Archaeology, vol. 1, no. 2, Ulster Archaeological Society, 1895, pp. 133–42, http://www.jstor.org/stable/20563549.
3) Irish Resurrectionism: 'This Execrable Trade', by Alun Evans, Ulster Journal of Archaeology, vol. 69, Ulster Archaeological Society, 2010, https://www.jstor.org
4) Disremembering 1798? An Archaeology of Social Forgetting and Remembrance in Ulster, by Guy Beiner (2013) History and Memory, vol. 25, no. 1, Indiana University Press, 2013, pp. 9–50, https://doi.org/10.2979/histmemo.25.1.9.; [This author was born and raised at Magherageery in the townland of Blaris, County Down. In my late 40s I happened to learn from a book (see ATQ Stewart above) that a field at Blaris, upon which I had played as a child and worked as a young man, had been the scene of a multiple execution - that of the four young United Irishmen, Peter Carron, Daniel Gillan, and the McKenna brothers *(2)*. After I wrote about this in the Irish Times (An Irishman's Diary, June 07, 2003) local people of all ages were as astounded as I had been.]
https://www.irishtimes.com/opinion/an-irishman-s-diary-1.361770
5) From a Down County Museum initiative to educate local schoolchildren on the Great Famine in Co. Down, www.downcountymuseum.com
6) https://premium.weatherweb.net/weather-in-history-1850-to-1899-ad/
7) The Hand-Loom in Ulster's Post-Famine Linen Industry: The Limits of Mechanisation etc, by Kevin J. James 2004,

https://franklinhslibrary.pbworks.com/w/file/fetch/99719951/mechanization.pdf
8) The Irish Potato Famine 1846-1850, Dochara: An Insider's Guide to Ireland, https://www.dochara.com/

A workhouse was the absolute last resort for starving people during Ireland's Great Famine

Chapter 1

To Newry

Early on the morning of Thursday, May 24rd 1855, John Adams folded a piece of cloth around some bread and a lump of cheese and put the little parcel into the inside pocket of his overcoat. He slipped his pipe and razor into another inside pocket. He then filled a bottle with cold tea, corked the top with a rag, and carefully placed it in an outside pocket so he could hold it upright as he went along. With that, having said a few farewells the previous evening, he left his home at Annahilt and set off to walk to Newry, some 31 miles away, to join the army. It would be many years, decades in fact, before he set eyes on Annahilt again. It was a bitterly cold day, well below freezing, and this had him striding along at a brisker pace than he normally would when setting out to walk so far. But at least it wasn't raining.

As he walked, John cast an occasional glance across the fields on either side of him. Not through any romantic sense of attachment or in admiration of their beauty. Rather, to casually assess, as country people tend to do, how the local farmers might be faring. He had spent too many years battling against the land, and most of what grew upon it, in an effort to eke out a living, to feel any sense of emotional attachment towards it. John would have argued that the only people who found beauty in fields were those who had never had to work them. He looked at the land in much the same way as a trawler man might consider a shoal of fish. While a non-fisherman would be marvelling at the beautifully synchronised movements of the fish, the trawler man would be imagining them lying bloodied on the deck of his ship, ready for gutting and selling.

The Ballynahinch Road out of Annahilt took John straight to Hillsborough, through which ran the main Dublin Road. This in turn went straight to Dromore, then Banbridge, and on to Newry. With a bit of luck, he might get a lift or two along the way. If not, he had allowed himself plenty of time, including for an overnight stop in one of the towns if the weather turned wet.

John's luck was in. He got two lifts. On the southern side of Hillsborough, an old man driving a donkey and turf-laden cart stopped beside John and motioned for him to climb aboard "and take the weight off your legs". He was happy to oblige. "That's another tight one," said John, referring to the weather. And, with a shiver, "Just as well I put the top-coat on." "It's just as well you have one," replied the old man, and they both laughed. After a short while, the old man glanced at him across the makeshift seat they were sharing, and asked, "Where are you off to then?" "I'm headed for Newry," replied John. "Ah, so it's the army then," said the old man, nodding knowingly. "It is indeed," said John.

They fell silent for a while, then the old man looked across at him again and, with the same knowing expression, said, "You'll be fine. Just as long you remember to always do what you're told, and never volunteer for anything." John smiled, "I certainly will." This old maxim wasn't new to him. He had heard it many times before. There were a sprinkling of old soldiers living in and around Annahilt, most of whom, at the first opportunity, would reminisce at length about their soldiering days. Each time one of them would air this line, or a variation on it, such as, "Keep your head down, and try not to be noticed", John would laugh and act as though it was the first he had heard it. The old man dropped him off on the outskirts of Dromore. "Remember what I told you, now," he said, as John climbed down from the cart.

Later, while sitting against a wall in Dromore, eating his lunch, he fell into conversation with a fellow around the same age as himself, who happened to be sitting close by. Thomas Maloney was his name. They chatted and complained about everything from the weather to the price of tobacco and stout. John offered him some bread and cheese, and mentioned that he was going to Newry to sign up for the army. "Time I was out of here. I'm sick of the place. Time to see a bit of the world," he declared with a flourish. Thomas told him that, "given the pickle I'm in", he would be doing exactly the same thing himself but for the fact that he had "too many mouths to feed". That is, he was married and had children. John did not enquire about the nature of the "pickle". If his companion wanted to tell him about it, he would. For the moment, all Thomas volunteered was that he and his wife and children were about to set off for Banbridge to stay with relatives for a while. He added that he would be happy to give John a lift that far. At this point a man approached, and slipped some money to Thomas, who then left, telling John to wait where he was while he collected his horse, cart and family.

After waiting for over an hour, John had given up hope of ever seeing his new-found friend again. Then, just as he was making ready to leave, suddenly round a corner Thomas came. He was driving an aged horse attached to an equally-aged cart, which was laden with various bits of furniture and numerous large bundles of what appeared to be rags. Scattered amongst and on top of these were a frightened looking woman and (as it turned out) four children aged between about two and eight years. Thomas, red in the face and looking flustered, beckoned for John to climb up quickly beside him, and off they set at a canter for Banbridge.

When they got beyond the town, Thomas relaxed and began to explain his situation and the need for such haste. He had worked for many years on a farm just outside Dromore. A cottage came with the job, and the rent for this was deducted from his wages. The farmer's son, "a lazy, good-for-nothing waster", aged about 20 years, had got a local girl "in trouble" and they intended to marry soon. He had only learned of this development a couple of days before when the farmer suddenly announced to him that the son would need his cottage and his job as he'll "soon have a wee family of his own to keep". He gave him a week to pack up his things and leave. When he met John in Dromore, Thomas had just finished selling some furniture that he'd taken from the cottage. Furniture that belonged to the farmer. While he was haggling with would-be buyers, his wife had gone back home with the horse and cart to load up whatever they could take with them, and prepare the children for travelling. Thomas was late getting back to John because he had decided to make a bonfire out of whatever they couldn't sell or carry. This included the front and back doors of the cottage. "I made certain that young bastard will be walking into an empty house with his wife," he declared, shaking with anger, "And he should thank me for making sure they won't have to open a door to get in or out of it, either. You break your back for them for years, and what thanks do you get? Thrown out on the street with your wife and wee'uns at a minute's notice, without a care whether you live or die."

He and the family were now headed for Ballyroney, near Rathfriland, to stay with the wife's brother until Thomas could get himself another job and somewhere for them to live. He said he intended selling the horse and cart when he got there, to keep them going in the meantime. "You didn't take the horse and cart, too," John enquired, somewhat tentatively. Stealing a few bits of furniture and bedding was one thing, but a horse and cart was something else altogether. Thomas laughed, "Nah, I'm not that daft. Sure these belonged to my aul fella, and when he died they came down to me." As they entered Banbridge, Thomas stopped the cart and dropped John off, before turning left in the direction of Katesbridge. "Good luck with the army. And if anyone asks, you didn't see us," said Thomas, and, with a wink and a wave, he and his family were gone.

John walked the remaining 16 miles or so to Newry, not sure whether or not he wanted another lift. When he got beyond Loughbrickland and gazed across the fields on either side of him, John could not have known that over to his left, in a townland called Creevy, lived a family called McMahon/MacMahon/McMann (this being long before working people needed to know how their name was spelt). And further along, much closer to Newry and again off to his left, in the townland of Turmore, lived the Lyons family. Even if he had at least heard of these two families, as they each had weavers amongst their number, he couldn't possibly have imagined that a shared descendant of theirs would play a pivotal role in the lives of descendants of his own.

It was early afternoon when John arrived in Newry, the self-styled Gateway to the North. Rather than waste any time, he headed straight for the local army barracks to speak with a recruiting sergeant. Newry was a big town, with a population of around 16,000 people, much bigger than John had anticipated, but he had no difficulty in finding the barracks. The first person he asked directed him straight to it. He spoke to a sentry at the main gate, a young Scottish fellow, who escorted him to the recruiting office.

There, sat behind a desk, was Sergeant Dobson, a large muscular man, about 5ft 10in tall. Dobson had the air of someone who was not normally given to niceties, but was making a huge effort on this particular occasion to create the impression that paternalistic affability and helpfulness came as natural to him as breathing. "So you want to join the army, son," he said in a regional English accent, while twisting his face into something resembling a smile. "Well, we can certainly help you there. Did you have any particular regiment in mind?" John said something about how he'd rather not join an Irish outfit, if possible. This was not, God forbid, an attempt to distance himself from or deny his Irishness. But, rather, he was motivated by a desire to leave personal aspects of his past as far behind him as possible. A non-Irish regiment would virtually ensure that he didn't find himself in the company of anyone who might know him.

Sergeant Dobson must have misheard John. He drew in his breath, ran his fingers through his carefully manicured moustache, as though in thought, and tutted loudly, "Well now, son. Can't help you with that, I'm afraid. You'll have to travel all the way to Dublin to join a Paddy regiment. And I'm not even sure if they're recruiting at the minute." This was a lie, on both counts, as John well knew. But even if Dobson had said that Irish regiments were crying out for soldiers, and were at this minute recruiting in Lisburn (both of which were true) John would have stayed where he was. He wanted - felt he needed - to get as far away as possible from his former life. And joining an Irish regiment could not guarantee that. He had come this far and just wanted to get the formalities over and done with, regardless of what regiment he joined, just so long as it wasn't Irish. Dobson didn't immediately pick up on how eager John was to join the army. Or maybe he did, but felt obliged nonetheless to drive on with the recruitment patter he had delivered countless times, to countless young men, in countless towns and cities across Britain and Ireland. "I've been in the army for 20-odd years, and I can tell you, son, there's no better life to be had. You'll be paid at least one shilling a day, and have your every need taken care of. You'll get to see the world, and never again know what it's like to go hungry. "If you behave yourself and do what you're told, there's a good chance of promotion, and the extra money that comes with it. Before I joined the army I was earning a pittance digging ditches in and around Coventry for a tight-wad reprobate whose name I won't even allow to cross my lips. But look at me now! And it's all down to the army. Thank God for the British army. And all that's ever asked of us in return is that we fight for Queen and Country when we're needed." As he went on and on in similar vein, Dobson began to remind John of a certain hawker he knew, an ever-present at Lisburn's Tuesday market.

An hour later, John had agreed to sign on for an initial period of 10 years to General Service (meaning he could be sent to any regiment that happened at that time to be in need of new recruits) but only after Dobson had consulted a pile of papers on his desk, and told him that he would be joining the 46th (South Devonshire) Regiment of Foot, and his regimental number would be 3708. (At the time, a soldier was given a *regimental* number, as opposed to an army number. If he subsequently changed regiment, he was given a new number.)

After the formalities were done, Dobson reached into his pocket and pulled out a shiny shilling (5p), which he grandly proffered to John as though indulging in an act of personal generosity: "Here you are, take this son. Report back to me first thing in the morning and we'll get you a medical, and have you sworn in by a magistrate." John nodded. Then, seemingly as an afterthought, the sergeant enquired: "Have you got anywhere to stay tonight, son?" John shook his head. "Well, I'd highly recommend old Mrs Twomey's place, she's just up the road from here on Barrack Row."

Mrs Twomey, who seemed like a friendly sort, was a tiny, rotund woman of ruddy face and indeterminate old age. Although a widow of many years, she nonetheless wanted for nothing; assured of a more-than-modest income on account of her lodging house being in such close proximity to the army barracks. That, and her mutually beneficial arrangement with Sergeant Dobson.

She offered John a choice between a shared bed for tuppence-halfpenny, and a bed of his own in a shared room for fourpence. He took the second option. For another halfpenny, she presented him with a cold supper of scraps of bread and mutton and a jug of water. It was too cold to explore the town, and anyway he'd had enough walking that day, so after supper John went straight up to his room.

He found that he was sharing with just one other man, a Declan MacNamee from Dublin. Neither was ready for sleep, so they struck up a conversation. "So what has you in this part of the world?" asked Declan. "I'm signing on to the army in the morning," replied John, "And yourself?" Well, it's certainly not the army. I'm here with my work. A seaman. Just waiting on a boat up to Belfast, and from there on to England then France. And God knows where after that," explained Declan.

John didn't ask why he hadn't just taken a boat straight from Dublin. Instead, something popped out of his mouth without warning, "You believe in God then, do you?" Declan thought for a minute, "I'm not sure, to be honest. I'm Catholic, so I suppose I should. But I never think about it. And now that I do think about it, I'm not at all certain. And yourself?" "I'm afraid not to believe," said John. "Well if you're afraid of what'll happen to you if you don't believe in God, then that must mean you do believe in Him," said Declan, "Otherwise, what is there to be afraid of?" "No, I didn't mean it that way," replied John, "I'm afraid of believing that this is all there is. This misery of a life that most of us lead. If I stopped believing that there might be something better than this beyond the grave, what would be the point of getting out of bed in the morning? Or what would there be to stop me from just robbing everybody I came across, rather than breaking my back to earn a shilling or two, if I don't believe I'll have to pay for my sins some day." "You sound like a very good Christian to me. I think you'll get to Heaven all right." said Declan, eager to bring the conversation to a close. John laughed, "I'm actually a very bad Christian, and I've no chance of making it to Heaven. But it's nice to think that if I change my ways it might still be possible." And, thinking of his late mother, "most of all, I like to believe that the people who deserve to get to Heaven, who've spent all their lives being genuinely good Christians, get their reward."

It was then that he realised what had sparked his question to Declan in the first place. The day before he'd been wondering what his mother would have thought of him joining the army, and whether she was looking down on him from Above. Whether in fact she had made it to the Above, as she surely deserved to. And then, whether there actually was an Above to get to. As those who knew John best would have said, "Oh, he can be a deep one all right."

He rose early the next morning, splashed some water on his face, and headed off to Newry Barracks as arranged. There he met with Sergeant Dobson again, who led him off for his medical. The medical was largely cursory, designed as much to detect the scars from flogging as it was to find any signs of illness or physical disability. It took only about 20 minutes to complete. After that, he went before a magistrate who had come to the barracks specifically for the purpose. John raised a Bible in his right hand and, repeating the words of the magistrate, swore his allegiance to Queen and Country.

So, on the morning of Friday, May 25th 1855, John Adams became a British soldier. And was made fully aware of that fact almost immediately upon its formal enactment. He had no sooner lowered the Bible than Sergeant Dobson dispensed with the fatherly act. "Right then soldier, no dilly-dallying there. You're in the army now, so let's be having you. Follow me," he bellowed, before turning on his heels and marching out of the room. John followed quickly behind him. As part of that morning's process, for the first time an abiding description of John Adams was put on record. He was 5 feet 6 inches tall, with blue eyes, brown hair and of a fresh complexion. It seems that brown eyes, dark complexion, and even darker hair had yet to enter the Adams gene pool.

Training

On the morning of May 26th, 1855, less than 24 hours after his enlistment, John and five other new recruits were taken by wagon from Newry to Belfast, put on a sailing boat for Liverpool, and told they would be met by some NCOs on the other side. The other lads, all younger than John, were from the south Down, south Armagh and Louth areas, and had been labourers of one kind or another. The only exception to this was a young fella from Newry, Paddy MacGowan, who described his previous occupation as, "beggin' on the streets of the town". Each member of the little group, including John, was gripped by a mixture of trepidation and excitement. They chatted nervously amongst themselves, off and on, throughout the near 36-hour voyage. At one point a passing deckhand remarked to them, "Geez lads, they must be in a quare hurry to get youse over. It's usually 50 to a 100 of youse we take at a time." The recruits laughed, and thought no more about it.

"Where did you say you were from again?" asked Paddy. "A wee place called Annahilt," John replied, "It's near to Hillsborough and Lisburn, maybe halfway between the two, but off to the east a bit from both."

"And what has you joining the army at your age?" Paddy went on. "I got sick of the flax," answered John, and, though he need hardly have asked, "And what about yourself?" "I got sick of the beggin'," laughed Paddy.

He went on to explain that his mother and younger sister had "died of the hunger" a few years back, and his father had "turned strange" as a result. The father finally wandered off and never came back, and Paddy had been fending for himself ever since. One day, a wee woman stopped with him, gave him a halfpenny, and suggested he join the army. He'd thought of that before, but was certain they wouldn't take him. "Leave it to me," she said, "I'll put a word in for you." And so she had, and here he was.

His mention of this woman rang a bell with John. "Tell me this," he asked, "Was she a wee heavy-set woman, with grey hair and a red face?" "She was indeed," said Paddy, "Why, do you know her?" "I think I've met her," laughed John. Paddy, short and stick-thin without a hair on his face, looked about fourteen at most. But there was no point in John asking him his age. He wouldn't have known what it was, anyway. Nor did he have any reason to know. It wasn't as if anyone in those days, outside of a highly-privileged few, took any notice of birthdays, much less celebrated them. What was there to celebrate? Most people had more important things on their minds, like where the next bite of food was coming from, to be bothered about their age. John himself, for example, knew that he was born sometime in the early part of 1830 (or was it 1829?) because his mother had told him so. But neither he, nor she, had any firm idea of which month he was born in, never mind on what particular day. It would be more than a decade later, 1864, before it became compulsory in Ireland to register births, deaths, and marriages. And many decades after that before it became unthinkable not to do so.

The ship docked at Liverpool on the afternoon of the next day, where the Irish contingent was met by a couple of army corporals. The corporals ordered them to join up with a larger group of 50 to 60 men standing off to one side, who looked as if they had been waiting around for a while. As soon as the Irish lads had joined the larger group, everyone was ordered on to wagons and taken to Lime Street railway station. From there they were sent by rail to army barracks at Aldershot in the southeast of England for their training.

The provision of wagons wasn't to save the recruits' legs, but to save the army's blushes. When in the past they'd tried to walk new recruits through Liverpool it was "like trying to herd Brown's cows" as one corporal put it. Worse still, local people would invariably stop to point and laugh at the gaggle of ill-dressed men and boys wandering along the middle of the street with less co-ordination and sense of direction than a flock of sheep. While red-faced corporals ran around like sheepdogs, barking orders in an attempt to organise and direct them. People would shout insults, such as "God help us if we're depending on the likes of this lot" and "where did they get this sorry bunch of scallies from, the workhouse". They would even start picking-out individuals from among the recruits, "look at that one there, he barely has a pair of shoes on his feet". It was soon decided that this wasn't the kind of image the army wanted to project, and they would be better off just hiring a few wagons instead.

John settled easily into army life. Though, like many a new recruit before him, for the first few days he felt the hardest part must be getting used to the uniform. Every piece of it was made of such rough fabric that he itched constantly. After a week or so, however, his skin became accustomed (or hardened) and the itching disappeared. The food was excellent - meat, potatoes and gravy at least three times a week - though Sergeant Dobson had neglected to mention that soldiers had to pay sixpence a day for their meals.

The recruits were housed in large barrack rooms, each to his own bed. For most of the younger lads this was the first time that they didn't have to share a bed with two, three, or even four siblings. And for others, it was one of the few times that they had actually had a bed to sleep in. At first the blankets itched just as much as the uniforms. But, as with the uniforms, this only lasted a few days. John particularly liked the sense of comradeship that quickly developed amongst his colleagues. There were lads from virtually every part of Britain, many of them from towns and villages that he had never heard of. But the similarities in their familial and social backgrounds far outweighed the geographical differences. This, and a common sense of need, if not yet of purpose, meant they bonded easily and quickly. In no time at all everyone was helping and looking out for one another. Well, except for one recruit, that is, who needed a little more encouragement that the rest.

Amos, from somewhere in the south of England, wasn't noticeably bigger than most of the other recruits, but he was older. And he liked to bully them. Nothing physical at first, just snide remarks and veiled threats, and generally shoving people around. The more Amos got away with it, the more he pushed his luck. He started sneaking up behind his favourite victims and punching them on the shoulder or upper arm. Then he moved on to demanding they give him food and tobacco. John slept in the same barrack room as Amos and had witnessed more than enough of his antics.

One evening, Amos sneaked up behind another recruit and grabbed him in a head-lock. John was sitting on his bed nearby, undoing his boots. As the young lad struggled, making choking noises and going redder in the face, Amos cackled with delight, loosening and tightening his grip, "Where's my tobacco, you little twerp." "I haven't got any tobacco, Amos," gasped the victim. John stood up, glared at Amos, and in a loud voice said, "Leave him alone, Amos. We've had enough of your bullying." Amos let go of the young fella, and glared back at John, "Mind your own business, Paddy. It's got nothing to do with you." "The name's John. Now stop the bullying or I'll put a stop to it," said John, calmly. Amos let out a nervous laugh, "You'll stop nothing, Paddy. Now go back to tying your boots. You've probably got them on the wrong feet, anyway. What with not knowing your left hand from your right." John drew out his fist and hit Amos full on the face, knocking him to the floor. Then he took a step forward and stood over him, looking down, "Correct me if I'm wrong, Amos, but I believe that was my right hand." Amos didn't speak, but just lay there looking up at John, blood trickling from his nose. "As I told you, let that be an end to your bullying," ordered John, before walking away. Amos decided that maybe bullying wasn't such a good idea, after all. The little band of six who had travelled over from Ireland stuck together for only a little while at Aldershot. Soon each of them made new friends, and was swallowed up in the crowd. John would occasionally bump into Paddy, and would always ask, "Well Paddy, how's it going?" More often than not, Paddy would answer with a grin, a nod, and an exaggerated rubbing of his belly.

Some of the accents were hard to understand at first, but John soon got used to them, just as others got used to his. It was hardly surprising that the Scottish and Irish had little difficulty in understanding one another. But both could struggle with a heavy southern English accent. And likewise the southern English lads often had difficulty understanding recruits from Scotland and Ireland. In fact they could hardly tell the accents apart. The common denominator was the Geordies, who everybody struggled to understand.

Most of all, John liked not having to worry about the things he had been able to push to the back of his mind during waking hours at home. But towards the end of his time at home they had begun sometimes to haunt him even while he slept: whether the flax would hold up, what sort of quality it would be, and, underpinning every other worry, where his next few pennies were coming from. He hadn't realised quite how much pressure he had been under at home until it was gone. From the moment he left the cottage at Annahilt, he began to feel less burdened and lighter of mind. By the time he reached Newry, he was even feeling a sense of freedom. He found this strange, seeing as he was now in the army. But then again, since joining the army every day had been ordered for him, and every decision taken by someone else. Now, on the rare occasions that he allowed flax to enter his mind, it was only to remind himself that he never wanted to lay eyes on it again. There were some things that he couldn't dismiss from his mind. Nor did he particularly want to.

The military training given to the troops at Aldershot was basic in the extreme. Essentially, they were taught rudimentary drill, how to march in step, what the commands being bellowed out by a training sergeant meant, and how to use a rifle. (The army had recently replaced the old Brown Bess musket with the new Enfield rifle. Quite an upgrade: the Enfield was sighted up to 1,000 yards, whereas the Brown Bess's accuracy was limited to 100 yards at best.) The rifle training posed no problem to rural lads, like John, who had been around firearms of various types most of their lives.

The drilling and marching took John a little longer to master, however. Still, he had noticed early on that no matter how bad he seemed to be at something, there was always at least one person who was worse. This helped put him at ease, which in turn helped him to master whatever he was having difficulty with. Soon he was as accomplished as any other recruit, and far more accomplished than some. He fell into an easy complacency. So much so that he sometimes found himself thinking, "And they're actually paying me for this?" Little did he realise that a rude awakening was on the immediate horizon. He would soon be left in no doubt what exactly it was that the army was paying him for.

One evening, in the middle of his fourth week at Aldershot, as the day's training came to an end, a drill sergeant bellowed out, "Listen up, men. All soldiers of the 46th Foot will pack their gear this evening. Immediately upon reveille in the morning, they will report with said gear to parade-ground D. Do not forget any of your kit. And DO NOT BE LATE". A similar order was being relayed to all other training units that had members of the 46th amongst them. "What's this about?" John wondered aloud. A Scottish voice came in reply, "I don't know, but I think I can guess. Crimea!"

The information on John Adams (JA) regarding his age, height, general appearance, date and location of enlistment to the British Army, his regiment(s) and regimental number(s), date of his despatch to England and later to Crimea, is taken from his British Army Attestation papers, https://www.fold3.com

Carried by The Illustrated London News *of December 16, 1848, "The Ejectment", portrayed an eviction scene in Ireland*

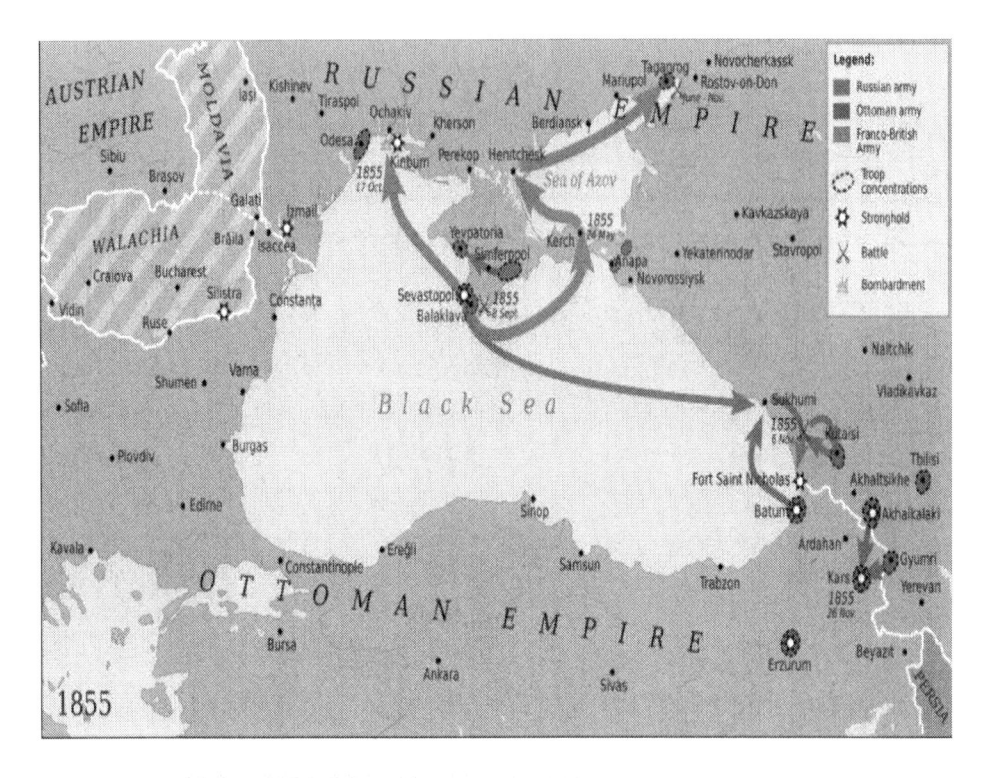

The 1855 positions of the Crimean war protagonists

Chapter 2
Crimea

The Crimean War lasted from October 1853 until February 1856. It was the scene of The Charge of the Light Brigade, and the selfless nursing of British soldiers by Florence Nightingale and Mary Seacole. It was notable too, according to virtually everything written about it afterwards, for being a prime example of notoriously incompetent international butchery. Which is quite an epitaph, given the incompetence and senseless butchery displayed in innumerable other fields of conflict before and after Crimea, but impossible to argue against.

The conflict was between Russia on one side, and the Ottoman Empire (Turkey), of which Crimea was a part, and Britain, France and Sardinia on the other. As always in these things, it was essentially a battle for territory and influence between some of the great powers of the time. The Ottoman Empire was in decline and Russia saw an opportunity to gain power and territory at its expense by exciting a war under the pretext of defending the rights of Christians (most especially, members of the Eastern Orthodox Church) in Palestine, which was also under Ottoman rule. For their part, Britain and France, fearing territorial expansion by Russia, and not without similar ambitions of their own, allied with the Ottomans. The war had finally centred on the Crimean Peninsula.

When John Adams arrived in Crimea, the eventual outcome of the war was still far from certain. The Russians had suffered military setbacks, but they were far from beaten. Sevastopol, a port city sitting on the Black Sea and the capital of Crimea, was strategically vital, and the Russians were determined to defend it at all costs. At least 30,000 Russian soldiers were holed up inside the walls of Sevastopol, under siege from the Allies. This city had become the Crimean Front. Although no one could have known it at the time, the war had entered its final year when John and some 80-odd of his colleagues from the 46th were sent there to augment the siege and bolster British army numbers. The final battle for Sevastopol had yet to come.

After 10 days sailing and a nine-hour overland hike, John and the other new arrivals mounted a small hillock and had their first sight of the periphery to the Crimean Front. Before them lay a sea of dark brown tents, their entrance flaps slapping and cracking like gunshots in the afternoon breeze. With depressing regularity, from a mile or so beyond the encampment came the deeper, comparatively muffled, sound of shells exploding, often followed by tiny earth tremors. As John and the other recruits got closer to the encampment, they were almost overwhelmed by the stench of human and equine excrement. When they entered its precincts, they were shocked by the state of the men and the animals they encountered. The place appeared to be mainly populated by living, breathing human skeletons clad in mud-covered outfits. Those who were not moving about stood or sat smoking in little groups, grunting and nodding in what passed for conversation. It was as if the very act of speaking was too exhausting.

Punctuating this scene were occasional strings of bedraggled dead-eyed horses, who stood tethered together in small groups with heads drooped and skins stretched tight across their rib cages. The tethering could only have been done out of force of habit, for it was obvious that the poor creatures had neither the energy nor the inclination to go anywhere. It struck John that there was something missing that added to the eeriness of the place. Something that should have been immediately obvious to him, but for a second or two he couldn't put his finger on it. Then he realised: there was no laughter or birdsong. "Good God Almighty," he thought, "have I died and gone to hell?"

The lance-corporal who was escorting the detachment stopped outside one of the tents, motioned to John and another man, a Derek Ransom from Coventry, and said simply, "Welcome to your new home." Then he and the rest of the men moved on, leaving John and Ransom where they stood. Ransom took a step back and motioned to John to enter first, which he did. As his eyes became accustomed to the gloom inside the tent, John saw there was a soldier lying in a corner, under some blankets. "How do?" said John, and motioned to a couple of straw-filled mattresses on either side of the tent, "Are these taken?" "No, help yourself, matey," the man replied, in a strong cockney accent, "The previous owners won't be needing them no more". Charles "Chirpy" Abbot, explained that there was only one other occupant of the tent at present, Jimmy Bradshaw, from Gloucester, who was "out in the trenches at the minute" and wouldn't be back for some time. Chirpy himself was on night duty, and was due back in the trenches again after dark. "Old Bradshaw's all right, but he ain't much company. Never speaks unless he has to. It's like living with a bloody monk," said Chirpy, "Of course it ain't always been like this. We've sometimes had up to a dozen men sleeping here. But they kept getting killed or wounded, the lucky sods." Chirpy had been in Crimea for 10 months, "a fucking hell-hole, matey", and would be happy to show them the ropes, if they liked.

John took a shine to Chirpy immediately, and knew they would get along. He had a tendency to make snap judgements on people soon after meeting them, and was almost invariably right in his positive assessments, though could sometimes be proved spectacularly wrong in his negative ones. As for Bradshaw, he thought he sounded a bit like Ransom, who likewise wasn't given to wasting words if he could possibly help it. "It'll be as much craic as a dummy's meeting when those two get together," he thought to himself.

Chirpy was in the middle of explaining that everything here, "and I mean everything", is in short supply, when a corporal stuck his head into the tent and called out to John, "Right Adams, you're down for trench duty tonight. From 18:00 hours tonight until 08:00 hours tomorrow morning. Tag along with Abbot here, and he'll show you the ropes." Chirpy grinned up at John, "Welcome to the Crimea, matey." After the corporal had left, Chirpy continued where he had left off, "We ain't got enough food for the men or the horses, not enough bandages or medicines, not enough ammunition or powder, not enough clothes or blankets, and the tents are shit. But other than that, everything's fine." He then turned half-around as if to go back to sleep, but turned back again and added, as if to put things in perspective, "At least we're better off than the poor old Turks. I ran into some of them last week, and they were so weak from hunger and lack of sleep they could hardly carry their muskets, the poor sods." And with that he turned away, pulled the blankets over his head, and went back to sleep.

As Chirpy had intimated to his new colleagues, the sudden demand on the British Army Commissariat (ie its logistics department) upon the outbreak of the Crimea War laid bare its woeful incompetence. Its staff were determined to follow every petty bureaucratic rule they could find, regardless of the cost in lives to those they were supposed to be furnishing with supplies. The only thing they never seemed to follow was the most basic rule of all, that of common-sense. As a result, the supply chain to Crimea (that is, the supply of fodder and equipment for the horses, and food, equipment, clothing and tents for the men) almost collapsed, leading to extended shortages. *(1)* Not even munitions were being sent in anything like the quantities needed to fight a war.

John was more relieved than apprehensive about his first stint in the trenches. He knew it would happen sooner or later, anyway. And who better to partner with than an old sweat like Chirpy. He settled down on his straw-filled mattress and tried to get some sleep himself. He awakened to someone shaking his arm, and telling him in a loud whisper it was time to go and "do our bit for Queen and Country". "Okay, Chirpy, I'll be right with you," he mumbled.

In the ink-black darkness, and without any form of light to guide them, Chirpy took them unerringly to the trenches, which lay about a mile from the tents. They lowered themselves in and crouched down. The trench was only about four-feet deep, so they would have to spend the night hunkered down, staring out into the dark. (It would be the early part of World War One before it dawned on military commanders that it might be better to dig their trenches twice as deep, to around eight feet, to allow sentries to stand upright and move around without fear of being seen and shot at by snipers.)

Chirpy told John what it had been like in the trenches during the previous winter: "I've never felt cold like it, matey. And hope never to again. Men would freeze to death where they sat. Oh yes, I saw that plenty of times. You'd speak to a chap and wonder why he didn't answer. Fucking froze to an icicle he was, that's why." And the tents weren't much better than the trenches, according to Chirpy, "It pissed rain or snow every day. But we might as well have been sleeping outside, for all the good the tents were. They leaked so badly, everything was soaked. Clothes, boots, blankets, men. Everything! Then a bloody great storm came and blew the lot away. What a winter, matey. What a bloody winter."

"Part of the reason I took the shilling was to get away from weather like that," remarked John. "And to see the world?" laughed Chirpy.

Chirpy wasn't exaggerating when he described what soldiers on all sides had been forced to endure the previous winter, and indeed throughout the Crimean War. At war's end, some 500,000 men had lost their lives, with the vast majority of these deaths caused by the terrible living conditions of the soldiers. *(2)* As the war progressed, diseases such as typhus, typhoid, cholera, and dysentery were rife, particularly in army hospitals.

Of the estimated 22,000 British casualties, 6,000 died in battle and the remaining 16,000 succumbing to illness or disease. The French suffered far worse than the British, with more than 95,600 men dying: 10,240 in action, 20,000 of wounds, and a mammoth 60,000 of preventable illnesses and disease.

The death rate for British soldiers sent to Crimea was 22.7 per cent; for French soldiers it was higher still at 30.9 per cent; and for Russian soldiers it was at least as high as for the French. By way of comparison, the death rate for future American soldiers sent to Vietnam was 2.3 per cent. *(3)* One can hardly begin to imagine how much higher the British death toll would have been without the work of Mary Seacole, Florence Nightingale and their fellow nurses.

"Listen up, matey," whispered Chirpy, "and tell me what you can hear." John listened for a moment, straining to hear what he had missed, then confessed, "I can't hear a thing, Chirpy." "Exactly! And that's why night duty is the best of the lot. The noise of the shelling here during the day is enough to drive a man cuckoo. That along with the constant worry of being hit by a sniper. I've seen men lose their heads over it. 'Trench madness' they call it. There's no telling what a man might do when he gets it. I think that's what's happening to old Bradshaw, if I'm honest. With him going so quiet an' all." "I'll have to try and pull night duty as much as I can, then," said John. "Stick with me, John. I'll look after that for you. I always get night duty, me," replied Chirpy. John knew better than to ask Chirpy how he managed to swing this. He settled instead for feeling extremely grateful, and noting that the cockney had addressed him by his name for the first time. Nor could he help but congratulate himself on how well he had judged the man from the instant they had met. "Thanks, matey," said John.

Chirpy was as good as his word, somehow ensuring that John was as regular a fixture on night duty as himself. Many times in later life, John would credit Chirpy with keeping him alive during the Crimean War, at least during the early months when he was still finding his feet. One night a Russian soldier must have got bored, or maybe cracked under the pressure, and began firing random shots in the general direction of the British trenches. This startled John, who immediately ducked down even lower in the trench. Chirpy, laughed, "Never worry about those poor fuckers over there. They're in as bad a state as we are. The Russians aren't the real enemy here. Our enemies are the weather and the sicknesses, and most of all the fuckers who have us here but can't be bothered to feed us properly or give us the proper gear. They're the real enemy."

When not overseas, a British soldier received two meals a day. In the morning a bread ration and tea or coffee, and for dinner a lump of raw beef or mutton. The meat would be boiled by the soldier, or his wife, and served in a broth. British soldiers overseas would receive portions of salted rather than fresh meat, shipped out from the UK, and hard biscuits rather than bread. The hardness of the biscuits meant they didn't go stale or mouldy, but it made them virtually inedible if they weren't first soaked in water, tea, coffee or some other liquid. The constant consumption of salted meat by overseas soldiers gave them a raging thirst, which they could hardly slake with the local water, which was invariably either scarce, contaminated or both. So they took to consuming alcohol in large quantities, most often spirits. Soldiers, whether based at home or abroad, would have to pay for their food rations, just as they had to pay for their uniforms, with the money being deducted from their wages. *(4)*

In Crimea, as Chirpy said, the Commissariat hadn't even managed to supply the men with the alcohol, never mind the food. Chirpy wasn't always successful at swinging night duty, and sometimes he and John would have to do a few days in the trenches during the hours of daylight. The difference between night duty and its daytime equivalent was stark. Frighteningly so. The day-sentries would take up position before daybreak and leave again after nightfall, to avoid being spotted by the Russians. Which was fine. It was the bit in between that ground down hard on the nerves. During the bombardments from either side, which could go on for hours at a time without stopping, conversation was rendered impossible. Such was the intensity of the bombing that no one left the trenches after a daytime stint without a pounding headache. But that was the least of it. The shelling posed a great danger to the men, of course. That was, partly at least, its purpose. John had never felt as helpless in his life, nor would he ever feel so again, as when crouched upon his knees, listening to the high-pitched whistle of a shell overhead, an indication that it was close to directly above, while hoping and praying that its final destination would be nowhere near his position. And that was the other part of the purpose of the shelling. To shred the nerves. And then there were the snipers. Any movement in the daytime trenches, however slight, was not undertaken without taking account of the danger posed by the snipers on the other side. If a sentry were to allow himself to start relaxing his guard, even in the slightest, he would inevitably become too complacent, and ultimately be shot by a sniper. This was the sniper's job, after all, to watch every movement of the men on the opposite side, and shoot them at the first opportunity. Nothing frightened the soldiers on both sides quite so much as snipers. And that, again, was partly their purpose, to keep the other side in a constant state of fear. When Chirpy had mentioned 'Trench Madness', John had understood what he meant, but only in an abstract kind of way. After experiencing day duty he was wondering to himself, "How does anyone not get Trench Madness, if they're stuck out here day after day."

Over the weeks that followed, Chirpy taught him how to roast and grind coffee beans in a used shell casing. When the coffee had been drank, the grinds could be dried and mixed with a little tobacco to fill a pipe, or be smoked on their own if needs be. An empty shell casing was useful too for catching rainwater, to save having to drink the muddy "piss water" that was making so many men ill. He also introduced John to a relatively steady source of meat.

One night in the trench, John nearly jumped out of his skin when something brushed past his leg. "Holy Christ, what was that?" he exclaimed. "It's a rat, matey," Chirpy explained, "Big buggers, aren't they. Don't worry, they have more than enough to eat about here. They won't bite unless you corner them, or you're dead. We'll have him or one of his chums for breakfast in the morning." John looked at him, thinking he was joking. "I could never eat a rat," he said with a shudder, "I hate the bastards." Chirpy chuckled, "That's what I used to say." Later that night Chirpy took a blanket and motioned for John to follow him. "Quiet now," he whispered. After crawling along the trench for a little while, Chirpy stopped, and remained motionless for a few seconds. Then all of a sudden he tossed the blanket low across the ground, came down on it with both knees, and punched down hard a few times. Smiling, he reached under the blanket and pulled out a dead rat, which he held up by the tail for John to see. "That's breakfast sorted," he said, and tucked it into his belt.

The next morning, when they got back to their tent, Chirpy set about skinning and gutting the rodent, which was the size of a small cat. John needed no instruction on how to prepare an animal for eating. He'd been catching and skinning rabbits since he was a boy. But the thought of eating a rat, of all creatures, made his stomach heave and sent shivers through him. When he had finished with the skinning and gutting, Chirpy skewered the carcass with a piece of stiff wire, and strung it across a low fire they had built in the tent. Every so often he would re-position the carcass to ensure it was cooking evenly. Within half-an-hour their meal was ready. Not wanting to offend Chirpy, John agreed to try "just a wee bit". He slipped a piece of meat into his mouth, had a few chews at it with mouth wide open, and swallowed. Now that doesn't taste too bad, he thought. Chirpy was staring at him, waiting for the verdict. "It tastes a wee bit like chicken, but stronger," John said, "I'll try another bit if you don't mind." Not only did John help consume the rat, when the meat was finished he helped suck every bit of marrow out of its bones. John was soon as active as Chirpy in catching rats, and became almost as good at it. He wasn't the first Crimean soldier, nor would he be the last, to discover that when army rations were in short supply, which was almost always, the rats were something of a godsend.

As summer gave way to autumn, a strange atmosphere developed amongst the men. They were beginning to dread the coming of winter. Those who had experienced the previous one feared having to go through another. And those who hadn't had heard enough stories not want to have to face one themselves. But it was more than that. It was to do with more, too, than having to scratch a living, quite literally, against a never-ending backdrop of deprivation, illnesses, and disease.

Something approaching a collective melancholia had descended upon the men, brought about by the sheer predictability of their every waking hour. They wanted something to happen. *Anything* to happen, no matter what it was, just so long as it distracted from the daily monotony of their lives. The siege of Sevastopol, of which they were part, had lasted almost a year. But still there was no sign of the situation changing. The men were beginning to have difficulty imagining life beyond Crimea. Better dead than sentenced to spend the rest of their days in this god-forsaken dump, was the almost universal feeling. When, without warning, things did begin to change, the men were delighted.

Attack on Sevastopol

Throughout the early months of 1855, the situation had in fact gradually eased somewhat for the British troops laying siege to Sevastopol. As soon as winter had ended, the Allies had worked to restore and construct supply routes to the front lines. The most important of these was a 24-mile railroad from Balaclava to Sevastopol. The opening of supply routes didn't necessary mean that the nature, as opposed to the quantity, of supplies markedly improved. London kept sending the wrong types of items. A case in point being the coffee beans alluded to previously. When sack after sack of green coffee beans began arriving at the stores at Sevastopol, the sergeant in charge was heard to remark to a colleague, "What in God's name are we meant to do with these? Use them as grapeshot?" Clothes, boots, and blankets became slightly more plentiful, but bandages, medicines, and proper foodstuffs continued to remain in short supply. The railroad did manage to deliver much needed munitions, some 500 guns and plentiful ammunition, which allowed the Allies to launch sustained bombardments of Sevastopol from June 1855 onwards. On the 7th of September they began their most severe bombardment to date. Over three days, more than 300 allied cannon fired 150,000 rounds of ammunition at the Sevastopol fortress, causing the Russians to suffer a daily casualty rate of between 2,000 and 3,000 men. With the intensifying of the bombardment, Chirpy had remarked to John, "Aye, aye, something's up here. We'll soon be going into battle." "It can't come quick enough for me," was John's reply, though in fact he was extremely nervous at the prospect. Day after day, week after week, the bombardments had continued, until the troops were almost deafened by them. The ground shook constantly under their feet. Finally, on the night of August 26, the men were told to prepare themselves and their equipment for battle.

"So it's tomorrow morning, then," remarked Chirpy to John, as they moved around the tent, getting their gear ready, "How you feelin', matey?" John didn't look up from what he was doing. "Scared," was all he said. Chirpy, who had been in battle before at Alma, Balaclava and Inkerman, glanced over at him, "That's normal. Only a madman wouldn't be scared before a tussle like we're facing." John was shocked, "What? You mean even you're scared, Chirpy?" "Shitting meself, matey," came the reply, "And I'd be mightily worried if I wasn't." Then he sat down on his mattress and motioned for John to join him: "Listen, this is the worst part. The waiting! Once it starts you won't have time to be scared. All you'll be thinking about is staying alive, and doing for the fucker who's trying to do for you. Now remember this and you'll be fine: whatever happens tomorrow, for God's sake don't try to get back to our lines unless we're ordered to. Otherwise, as sure as we're sitting here, one of the NCOs or an officer will shoot you, or stick you like a pig, for desertion. And we don't want that to happen now matey, do we."

The next morning, just before dawn, the men stood lined up, waiting for the order to advance. Line upon line of white-faced soldiers stood staring out into the gloom in front of them, each with only one thought in his mind, "For God's sake give us the order, and let's get this over with." The noise of the bombardment was even more deafening than usual, the shaking of the ground beneath their feet even more pronounced. They would remain standing in line for a lot longer yet. It wasn't until noon that the bombardment ceased and the order was finally given to attack. On the 8th of September, 60,000 men of the allied forces launched a full-scale assault on Sevastopol. Little more than three calendar months after he joined the army at Newry, John Adams was going into battle.

The cavalry led the British charge, swords held aloft, with the infantry following close behind. They were headed for the Great Redan, the British objective. As they went forward the troops came under withering fire from the Russians. John and Chirpy, running side-by-side, saw men and horses begin to fall. Some had only stumbled and quickly regained their footing, but most stayed on the ground wounded, sometimes fatally. The squealing and screaming of horses and men could be heard above the gun and cannon fire. Still the men charged forward, led from the front, it must be said, by their junior officers and NCOs. Finally they got close to the Great Redan, and the fighting really began. The Russians were well dug in, and determined to hold out. As the two sides came together, every man fought with whatever was available or handiest to him. Fists, feet, bayonet, sword, rifle butt, gunshot - whatever it took to keep him alive. A canopy of gun smoke hung like an early morning Irish mist over the scene. From beneath and among the fog came a cacophony of shouting, screaming, and shooting. Many of the cavalry were now on their feet, after being dragged from or having their horses shot from beneath them. Swinging their swords, lopping off an enemy hand here and an arm there, or driving their blade through a midriff. But swords were no match for guns, and many of the cavalry were themselves cut down. Suddenly out of the corner of his eye, John saw a Russian raise a gun to point in his direction. Without thinking, and all in one movement, he spun half-around, raised his rifle and let loose a shot. The man's head exploded like an overripe tomato hit with a hammer. John felt nothing. Not pity, elation, relief, or fear. Nothing. His mind was a blank. The animal instinct to survive had taken him over completely. As he began to move forward, he felt a blow to one side of the back of his head, and turned quickly around. A Russian, much smaller than himself, had tried to club him with his rifle. But John's movement had, inadvertently, rendered it only a glancing blow. John raised his own rifle and, with all of his strength and weight, brought the butt down squarely on top of his attacker's head. The Russian collapsed in a heap, and lay still, face upwards, on the ground. John brought the rifle butt down twice more, hard on his face. The first time letting out a scream that he wasn't aware he had emitted. With a swift glance around him he moved on again. Ahead, and slightly off to the left, he spotted Chirpy, who he hadn't seen since soon after the hand-to-hand fighting began. He pushed and fought his way through the tussle and turmoil until he reached his friend's side. "You all right?" mouthed Chirpy, nodding at the blood running down the side of John's face and into his collar. He hadn't realised that he was bleeding. "It's nothing," he mouthed back. And they both returned to the fray. The Russians fought like tigers, but so too did the British, who managed finally to take and occupy the Great Redan. But their victory was only temporary. The French failed to launch a planned attack to ease pressure on the British troops. Realising that the British were being left exposed, the Russians prepared to mount an assault of their own to try to retake the Great Redan. They lined up 3,000 bayonet-wielding troops in full view of the British. At this, the British commander ordered his troops back to a ditch in front of the Great Redan. His men, still under sporadic attack from the Russians, had been fighting all afternoon and were by this point exhausted and running low on ammunition. They had held their objective for a little over two hours, at a cost on the day of 385 men killed, 176 missing, and 1,886 wounded. Although the British had failed to hold the Great Redan, it didn't matter in the overall scheme of things. The French, under a General Mac-Mahon, had managed to take two other key strategic positions from the Russians, the Malakoff redoubt and the Little Redan. The capture of these rendered the Russian defence of Sevastopol untenable. By the next morning (September 9th) the Russians had abandoned the southern side of the city. The Crimean War was not over, but the fall of Sevastopol determined that it soon would be. And also who would be the victors.

(5) Late on the night of September 8th, a few hours after the day's battle had come to an end, Chirpy and John were sat together in a ditch, bloodied but relatively unscathed. "So we made it then, John," Chirpy remarked to his friend. "We did indeed, Chirpy. We did indeed. Just a pity we couldn't hold on to the prize," replied John. Chirpy pointed to the bandage wrapped around John's head, underneath which was a gash some four inches long, "We held on to our lives, matey. And that's all that matters. The French were never going to come to our aid. And it probably would have been no different if it had been them waiting on us for help. The commanders are the same, on every side. Chasing after personal glory. And if they can't get the glory for themselves, they make damn sure some other sod doesn't get it." He waved a hand at the hundreds of their comrades scattered around them, "And they couldn't give a tuppenny damn what happens to us. We're only here to chase their glory for them." John laughed, "You've a great way with the words, Chirpy." Quick as a flash, back came Chirpy, in a poor imitation of an Irish accent, "Sure 'n' begorrah do you think so, John?" At this, John collapsed in a fit of laughing, "I've never in my life heard such a sorry attempt at an Irish accent. And I've never, ever heard an Irish person say begorrah." This set them off, laughing and joking about the silliest of things, late into the night. Two soldiers just glad to be alive.

After Sevastopol had fallen, both sides knew it was all but over. The hostilities continued for six months or so, while a truce was hammered together, but these were limited to skirmishes and sniper fire. The interregnum between the fall of Sevastopol and the formal ending of the war was a particularly stressful time for Allied and Russian troops alike. Everyone realised that the war was effectively over, but men were still being killed, albeit in far fewer numbers. And each man knew that he still risked suffering that fate. A niggling voice at the back of every mind was saying, "Wouldn't it be just my luck to make it this far, only to be killed when the finishing line is in sight." John was destined to experience a Crimean winter, regardless of the fall of Sevastopol. But, as Chirpy never tired of telling him, it wasn't nearly as hard on the men as the previous winter had been. Not only was the weather a little kinder - for the Crimean Peninsula, that is - but a combination of better supply lines (most especially the railway line), a marked lessening in hostilities, and, most critically, London finally sending more appropriate supplies in greater quantities, conditions were eased somewhat. Soon, plentiful supplies of foodstuffs - along with decent tents, blankets, boots and clothing - began to arrive at the front. There were still sporadic outbreaks of illnesses and disease, but these were much less than before.

Despite the marked improvement in their living conditions, with the threat of being killed playing on everyone's mind, the winter of 1855-1856 still felt never-ending to the men. But end it did, of course. And with spring, or near enough to it, came the news that everyone had been waiting for - a truce had finally been agreed and signed between the protagonists. The Paris Treaty, of March 30th 1856, brought the Crimean war to an end.

John had spent nine months on the Crimean Peninsula, and was subsequently awarded the British Crimean Medal to signify that he had been there. His medal came with a silver clasp with Sevastopol inscribed upon it. The clasp was to indicate that he had been in combat, and the inscription was a record of where that combat had taken place. Chirpy's Crimean medal carried four silver clasps on its ribbon, for Alma, Balaclava, Inkerman and Sevastopol. John and Chirpy also received The Turkish Crimean War Medal, awarded by the Ottoman Sultan as a show of appreciation to all surviving British, French and Sardinian troops who had fought in the war. Somewhat strangely, only survivors were awarded the Turkish Medal. The Sultan did not think to make post-humous awards to the next of kin of the Allied soldiers who had died at Crimea. Some of the British recipients, though John and Chirpy were not among them, were presented with Sardinian versions of the Turkish medal after a consignment of the British version was lost at sea in a shipwreck.

John and his comrades in the 46th had barely finished celebrating the Paris Peace Treaty before they had something else to celebrate. On May 11 1856, the 46th received orders to make ready for posting to Corfu. A week later, on May 18, John was among two companies of the the regiment that boarded the steamship Ripon at Balaclava. The Ripon set sail at 04:00 am the next morning for Corfu via Constantinople (Istanbul), and arrived at its destination at 02:00 pm on May 23rd 1856. Chirpy was not among those who travelled, for his soldiering days were nearly at an end. He had less than eight months left of a 10-year stint with the army, and, having declined to sign on again, was being posted back to England to see out this last period.

It was with genuine sadness that John bade him farewell before leaving for Balaclava, "I'm going to miss you, Chirpy. You've been a great friend to me. I probably wouldn't have survived Crimea if it weren't for you looking out for me." And then with great solemnity, he added, "I owe you my life." Chirpy laughed, "You owe me nothing, John. I only showed you what others showed me at the beginning. I knew you were a good sort from the moment I laid eyes on you. And I wasn't wrong." They shook hands, then hugged, and then shook hands again. "Look after yourself, matey. And be sure to look me up if you ever find yourself near the Mile End Road in London. Call in at the Black Bull pub, the people there will point you in my direction." "I will, Chirpy. I surely will. I'll make a point of it," John promised. And with that they parted, never to lay eyes on one another again.

Corfu

Corfu is the largest and northernmost of the Ionian Islands, which lie off Greece's west coast in the Ionian Sea. Just like its neighbours, it was and remains populated almost entirely by Greek people. Corfu was a British protectorate in 1856 and would remain so until 1864, when it finally achieved its natural position in the world, and joined with the rest of Greece. As part of its protective duties, Britain had troops stationed on the island, hence the deployment there of the 46th. They were stationed close to the capital, Corfu Town, at a barracks adjoining the New Fortress, to the west of the town. The New Fortress was far from "new" even in 1856, having been built between 1576 and 1654. It was so named to distinguish it from Corfu's Old Fortress, which was rebuilt in the 15th century on the site of a former Byzantine castle. The history of Corfu, from ancient times and before, is replete with battles, conquests, victories and defeats. Most real, and some invented. The evidence of this martial history is reflected in its architecture. To this day, extensive fortifications, ancient and not quite so ancient, surround the town and indeed the island.

There was another ancient reality to Corfu that still existed when John Adams landed there, and still exists to some degree today. Although it took no structural form, it was more solid and seemingly indestructible than all of the castles and forts put together. This was the antipathy (nay, deep-seated hatred) the population of the island felt towards anything remotely connected to Turkey, most particularly Turkish people. John was treated to an insight into the depth of this hatred soon after he arrived.

John didn't have many dealings with Turkish troops while he was in Crimea. But occasionally he would be detailed to work alongside some of them on mundane tasks such as making minor repairs to a road, helping unload a wagon, or collecting fodder for the horses. Although the Turks were a bit standoffish at first, as if judging him before committing themselves, they soon became very friendly, greeting him with, "Mirhaba", whenever they met. They would offer John little bits of food, and a few strands of tobacco when they had any. This may not sound like very much, but in the context of the Crimea, food and tobacco were like gold dust. None of the Turkish soldiers spoke a word of English, and it need hardly be said that John spoke no Ottoman Turkish. But they were able to communicate effectively enough by means of hand-signals, gestures, smiles and nods. John liked the Turks, they reminded him in many ways of country people back home. The mistake John made in Corfu was to mention this during a conversation with a couple of locals. At a loose end one Saturday afternoon, John decided to explore the town. He wound up in a bar, and soon fell into the company of two local men, both of whom had a smattering of English. The three of them began drinking together.

As one of his new-found friends handed him another beer, accompanied by yet another greeting, "Welcome to our island, my friend." John responded in slow deliberate English, "You are very good," and then, with the casual exaggeration typical of those who have had a few drinks too many, "You remind me of some very good Turkish friends of mine." Upon which, his new-found friends suddenly became new-found enemies. "Turkish? Fucking Turkish?" the recent beer provider exploded, and promptly spat on the floor. His other erstwhile drinking companion went further, grabbing John's beer and smashing it on the floor close to where his friend's spit had landed. Both of the islanders stepped back and raised their fists, about to give him a beating. They were ranting in Greek, the only word of which John understood was "Turk". Luckily the owner of the bar, a brute of a man, and his equally large son, were not so easily offended - or perhaps they feared the prospect of a large number of British soldiers visiting the bar afterwards, bent on wreaking revenge for what was about to happen to their colleague. Whatever the reason, they came swiftly to John's rescue. While the father held back the two locals, the son grabbed John by the scruff of the neck, tossed him out into the street, and locked the door behind him.

As he made his way back to the barracks, John made two mental notes to himself: Never again would he drink outside the company of colleagues from the 46th; and never again would he praise Turkish people if there was a Greek person within earshot. Other than that little incident, which John put down to his own naïveté, he generally found the people of Corfu to be very courteous and friendly. Much like *some other people* he had met on his, albeit thus far limited, travels.

Corfu was a very welcome respite for the men of the 46th. It was sunny, quiet, and peaceful. The food was good and plentiful, with never any shortage of fruit, vegetables, and meat to be had. And to sleep in barracks, never mind beds, after so long spent in cold, windswept, rain-soaked tents, felt like the height of luxury. Their official duties were equally relaxed, consisting almost entirely of sentry duty, drill, some rifle training, and an occasional foot patrol around the town. Though to what particular purpose the last of these was intended no one knew, including the officers and NCOs. "Just goin' for a wee dander up the town," John would announce, not inaccurately, when about to go out on patrol.

Groups of soldiers would sometimes be put to general maintenance jobs around the barracks: painting, gardening, minor structural repairs and the like. Corfu allowed the men to relax, recuperate and recharge their batteries after Crimea. And that essentially was the purpose of the posting. A reward for what they had been through. There was even a marked change in the attitude of the officers and NCOs, who were far less demanding than was normally the case. This was hardly surprising, since most of them had been at Crimea too. Some of them were there almost from the start of the war until its finish, and were as deserving of a rest as anyone - and more deserving than most.

In their leisure time the men would play cards, drink, and chase women (though without catching many, it must be said). And they gossiped, of course. They gossiped incessantly. A favourite topic throughout 1856 were the courts martial (two of them) in London of Lieutenant James Edward Perry, a junior officer of their own regiment. The military trials had actually taken place two years earlier, in July and September of 1854, and had attracted enormous public interest, due to the coverage afforded them by British newspapers, particularly *The Times of London (6)*. But the news and details of them were only now, post-Crimea, filtering down to most of the lower ranks.

Unlike the vast majority of army officers at the time, Lieutenant Perry of the 46th had not bought his officer commission, but, the son of a tradesman, had been recommended to the regiment by a friend of his father's. This, allied to his "low-born status" and his being very good at the job, marked him out from the beginning. Perry had been subjected to severe bullying by fellow officers, particularly a

Lieutenant Thomas Greer. Eventually he could take no more and attacked Greer with a silver candlestick, knocking him unconscious.

On the night of the attack, both men were in the Officers Mess of the 46th at Windsor. Greer bullied Perry into gambling with him: first at billiards, then pitch-and-toss, and finally at cards. But Perry beat him every time. Later that night, Greer had gone to Perry's room on two occasions, dragged Perry out of bed and demanded they play some more cards. But still Perry won each time. Finally, when Greer burst into his room a third time, and began trying to pull him out of bed again, Perry decided he had had enough. He reached behind his head, grabbed a silver candlestick, and brought it down on Greer's head. Greer was carried from the room, bloodied and unconscious, by other officers. The next day Perry was brought before the Commanding Officer of the 46th, charged with striking a fellow officer and sent for court-martial. This, in itself, was extremely rare. It was far from uncommon for officers to come to blows in the mess, and the usual punishment would have been a severe dressing down and a fine. But not this time.

Perry's first court-martial was held in early July, and from the outset was the subject of, largely adverse, coverage by *The Times of London*. This, in turn, helped set the mood of the public. It was clear from the beginning of the trial that the verdict and sentence were a foregone conclusion. Officer after officer took the stand to contend that they had never witnessed any bullying of Lieutenant Perry, and certainly not by Lieutenant Greer. In fact, they claimed, on the night of the assault both men had appeared very friendly with one another, playing billiards and cards together.

Perry was duly found guilty and sentenced to be cashiered (ie dismissed from the army in disgrace). The newspapers and the public were outraged. This did not pass the attention of Queen Victoria, who was required to sign off on the sentence, which she refused to do. For short a while it looked as if justice would be done by Lieutenant Perry, after all. But the army was not to be so easily swayed. Perry was tried again in September, on largely technical and trumped up charges, found guilty, and required to sell his commission and leave the army. It must have been cold comfort to him that Greer, whose true character was exposed during the second court-martial, was also forced to sell his commission. The British public was outraged, yet again, but not nearly so much as the ordinary soldiers of the 46th when news of the affair eventually filtered down to them. "The bloody bastards," declared Fletcher, a private who hailed originally from Liverpool,"They couldn't bear to have an ordinary working lad as their equal. Bloody toffs, the lot of them." Perry wasn't quite a "poor working lad" but Fletcher's general point was a good one. However, not all the points made were as sound: "Our good Queen, God bless her, tried her best for him, but they wouldn't listen even to her," growled another old sweat. He was obviously unaware, and likely wouldn't accept it even if told, that Queen Victoria was probably swayed more by public (and newspaper) opinion than by any sense of fair play.

Even the NCOs would occasionally speak out on the Perry affair within earshot of the men. A Lance-Sergeant went so far as to say directly to a couple of the men one night while they were on guard duty, "The poor lad. It's just not right. Just not right, at all." The story grew in the telling, of course, and it soon became "the stone-cold gospel truth" that Greer was "a wrong'un" and had been trying to sexually assault Perry and that's why he kept entering his room. By this account, Perry, not wanting to sully the good name of the army, didn't disclose any of this in an open court-martial, "but the nobs knew. They knew all right, but went ahead and convicted him anyway". This was totally untrue, of course. And, in fact couldn't have been further from the truth. It had emerged during the courts-martial that Greer had been sharing his bed with "a woman of ill-repute" on the night of the assault, and this helped the army decide, or find an excuse, to get rid of him. The rumour probably began because it had been reported that Greer was carried "part naked" from Perry's room after the assault. But this was hardly remarkable, considering it was the early hours of the morning when Greer had left his own bed (and his "woman of ill-repute") in a rage and he hadn't taken the time to change out of his night clothes.

If the commanding officers even noticed it, which is doubtful, the outrage of the men of the 46th was of far less concern to them than that of the general public. Right across the upper echelons of the British Army there had been a raising of eyebrows and much muttering about the damage being done to the image of the military by the Perry courts martial. To put it bluntly, the upper echelons didn't give a damn what ordinary soldiers thought. The Perry affair eventually faded from the minds of public and soldiers alike. But, where the second was concerned, it took a very long time for it to dissipate entirely. Finally, after two years and five months of sunning themselves on the island paradise of Corfu, on June 20th, 1858 the 46th received orders that they were to move out. And, on September 01, after their replacements had arrived and taken up position, they boarded the good ship *Urgent* in readiness for embarkation later that day. John Adams was on his way to India. *(7)*

1) Starving Their Own Men: Britain's Epic Supply Failure in the Crimea, by Andrew Knighton, June 24, 2017,
https://www.warhistoryonline.com/history/starving-men-britains-epic-supply-failurecrimea-mm.html
2) Encyclopaedia Britannica https://www.britannica.com/event/Crimean-War
3) Journal of the Royal Statistical Society: Series A (2014) 177, part 3, by Lynn McDonald, University of Guelph, Canada
4) A 19th Century British Soldier's Diet, by Dr Aoife Bhreatnach, February 11, 2016,
https://betheheroofyourownkitchen.wordpress.com/2016/02/11/a-19th-century-british-soldiers-diet/
5) Crimea: the War That Didn't Boil, A. J. P. Taylor, History Today, Volume 1, Issue 2, February 1951
6) The Times of London (July and September 1854) and various
7) As per JA's Army Attestation papers; 46th (South Devonshire) Regiment of Foot, National Army Museum Royal Hospital Road, London SW3 4HT

Other Sources: *The Ottoman Centuries: The Rise and Fall of the Turkish Empire, by Lord Kinross, published by William Morrow 1977; The Ottomans: Khans, Caesars and Caliphs, by Marc David Baer, published by Basic Books London, 2021*

An artist's impression of the final Battle for Sevastopol

Chapter 3

To India

At approximately two o'clock on the afternoon of Wednesday, September 01, 1858, the men of the 46th were marshalled aboard the steamship, *Urgent*, at Corfu, to begin their journey to India. They were to take what was deceptively referred to as "The Overland Route". This in fact would entail them travelling by ship as well as by rail, donkey, and foot before they reached their destination. Not counting officers, the travelling party consisted of 791 men and NCOs. Of these, 53 of the men were under guard, or effectively prisoners, presumably for relatively minor infractions. At 6:00 am the next morning, on September 02, the ship left Corfu harbour and the men of the 46th were on their way. The weather, by all accounts, was lovely. But then again, when is the weather not lovely in Corfu?

Their first destination was the Mediterranean port of Alexandria, in Egypt. Which they reached without incident three days later, on Sunday September 05, at about 5:00 am. It was much hotter in Alexandria than it had been in Corfu, and after the ship had docked there being no orders issued to disembark, the men lounged about on deck in the hot sun. The next day, September 06, there were still no orders, so everyone passed the morning as they had done the day before, lounging about under a scorching sun.

Bread and meat were delivered to the ship. The bread was fine, but the meat was rotten and totally inedible. This didn't go down too well with the men, who were beginning to lose patience with all the aimless hanging around. In the early afternoon the captain of *Urgent* ordered everyone below decks to allow for some refitting work to be carried out. The men grumbled but they obliged him, for a while. After sweltering below for more than an hour, they began cursing and complaining. By the time another hour had passed and there was still no sign of them being allowed back on deck, they'd had enough. "To hell with this, and to hell with the captain," shouted an old soldier, "I'm going back on deck whether it suits him or not. Who's with me, lads?" There were no shortage of volunteers. The men forced their way up through the hatchways and back on to the deck while the captain and his crew looked on, helpless to stop them. This mini-mutiny resulted in two companies of the 46th being denied "smoking privileges", but it appears to have worked. The next day there were no restrictions placed on the men's movements.

The wait for orders went on for a full 10 days after the *Urgent* had arriving in Alexandria, with everyone killing time on board ship as best they could. At last, in the early afternoon of September 15, the long-awaited order to disembark having finally arrived the previous morning, the 46th began to leave the ship. The leaving of Alexandria itself would be staggered. The regiment was split into two companies of 400-odd men. One company would set off immediately and the second would leave the next day. Much to his relief, John was in the first company.

A train was waiting, fired up and ready to go, near to where the men disembarked. Soon they were loaded up and on their way to Cairo. They were now kitted out in summer clothing - white trousers, light tunics, and forage caps with a neck flap to guard against the sun - which had been provided to them while they were waiting on the ship (each man would have to pay for his new uniform, of course. With the price deducted from his wages). It could hardly be said, though, that the men were travelling lightly. As they boarded the train, each was carrying his regular kit in a haversack, his greatcoat over one shoulder, and had a water bottle strapped to his side. This and being packed close together in the carriages, meant the men were soon almost stifled by the heat. Neither, as the train trundled along, was there any relief to be had from the open windows. The air coming through them from the outside felt every bit as hot as that on the inside. "I swear, I'll be roast beef before this is ended," grumbled John at one point. "If nothing else then, at least the rest of us have a decent meal to look forward to," a companion replied.

It wasn't long before the train itself began to struggle. Every so often its metal wheels would overheat and threaten to set fire to the wooden panelling above and around them. Several times they had to halt so the wheels and the woodwork could be doused with water. Eventually, five hours after setting off, the journey having taken two hours longer than it should have done, they were able to leave the train. They had reached the Nile River. "So this is what it looks like. Keep your eyes peeled for a wicker basket," remarked someone, as if to prove that the many boyhood hours he'd spent in Sunday School hadn't been entirely wasted.

A bridge over the Nile was under construction, but not yet finished, so the company crossed the river on barges and a steamship. On the other side they were given something to eat, and then immediately boarded on to another train, headed for Cairo. It was a little after 8:00pm, and slightly cooler than it had been earlier in the day. So although this train journey could hardly be described as comfortable, the journey was a lot less uncomfortable than the previous one. They arrived in Cairo at midnight and left almost immediately on yet another train. It wasn't long before their good fortune ran out again. About 10 miles beyond Cairo the train engine gave up, and they were forced to wait around for an hour until another one was sent to them. They then travelled onward, stopping only briefly for breakfast, to where the rail line ended. The end point was in the middle of the desert, as this railway was under construction too. They reached their desert destination about 8:30am on the morning of September 16th. And there awaiting them was their next mode of transport, donkeys.

One wag shouted upon seeing the donkeys, "I see lunch has been arranged, then. We're having overgrown rabbit, so plenty for all." Every one of them had seen donkeys before, of course, but not everyone had ridden one. Soon the donkeys had been loaded with baggage and men, and the little caravan set off into the desert, the donkeys being chided along by their Egyptian owner and his helpers, presumably family members. Donkeys do not like to be rushed, they much prefer to plod along at their own pace, particularly when labouring under a scorching desert sun. This lot were no different. They were prepared to take some chiding from the owner and his sons, who they were familiar with, but on no account would they accept it from the strange-smelling strangers now astride them.

Those amongst the 46th who had some dealing with donkeys knew this. So they just sat back and relaxed, and let the owner and his animals adopt whatever pace suited them. However, those who hadn't any such experience would insist on trying to push the donkeys to walk faster, nudging them in the ribs with their heels and pushing at their necks. The donkeys were having none of it. Every so often, after one nudge or push too many, an animal would rear up on its front legs, as if trying to do a handstand, and send its passenger flying over its head and into the roasting hot sand. It must have happened six or seven times before lessons were learnt. And each time it did, the men found it hilarious. "You'll never make a jockey," shouted a tiny man from Tipperary at one victim. "Just like yourself, then," was the huffy reply. "God, but there's some size of birds in this desert," shouted another wag, "But they're not too good at the flying."

The ribbing and banter went on throughout the long trek across the desert, lightening what would otherwise have been a tortuous journey. Over the course of 16 hours the donkeys carried them the same number of miles, until they finally reached their goal, Suez, in the early hours of the morning of September 17. They marched through the town, a welcome stretching of the legs after the donkey ride. At the the Suez dockside they were taken by steamer out to the *Precursor*, a P&O vessel lying in wait five miles out in the harbour. After a decent meal they bedded down for the night, without blankets, on the deck of the ship. Blankets or not, none of them needed rocking to sleep. The next day, at 12 noon, they were joined by their colleagues from the second company. And the day after that, September 18, most of the regiment was transferred to the steamship, *Oriental* (250 men had to be left behind on the *Precursor*, to follow later. The *Oriental* not being large enough to carry everyone). With all eligible men on board, John Adams amongst their number, they set sail for Aden at 9:00pm.

Food on board the *Oriental* was remarkably good. On alternate days, the men had either salted beef and preserved potatoes, followed by rice and plum duff, or salted pork with potatoes and rice and pea soup. Tea and biscuit were served every morning and evening. Measures of arrack, an alcoholic spirit made from cocoa sap or rice, were served a couple of times a day. The men of the 46th had seldom had it so good. A daily routine was soon established. Everyone would rise at 5:00 am, strip off and wash themselves down under the water from an engine-room hose. They would then wash the decks until breakfast at 8:00 am. At 11:00 am they fell-in for parade, before having dinner at 1:00 pm. After dinner, the first arrack of the day was served. Tea would be at 5:00 pm and, after a drummer had played a tattoo, at 9:00 pm it was time for bed. On account of the heat down below, everyone slept on deck, beneath their greatcoats to guard against mosquitos. (It gives an idea of the heat below decks when it was more comfortable to sleep under a greatcoat outside.) Every third day the men rose an hour earlier, at 4:00 am, to wash their clothes. The donkey ride would long be remembered, and talked and joked about by the men of the 46th. However, chief among their memories of the journey from Corfu to India would be an encounter they had while on the *Oriental*.

One morning, while John was helping wash down the decks, there suddenly began a great excitement off to his left. He turned to see a crowd, growing larger by the minute, lined up along the railing shouting, whooping, and pointing out to sea. He ran over and pushed his way to the front. He could not believe his eyes. There, about 100 yards out to sea, were hundreds upon hundreds of fish, flying through the air like birds. "What in God's name are they?" he asked. The failed jockey from Tipperary was sure he had the answer, "The fish and the birds must be mating with each other about these parts. It's the only thing that explains it." "Nonsense," rejoined someone further along the railing, "They're obviously birds that disguise themselves as fish for the hunting. Mr fish doesn't know it's a bird until it's too late, and he's being swallowed alive." All the while, oblivious to their audience, the flying fish were swooping gracefully in and out of the water, wings outstretched, like a host of little silver aquatic ballerinas. The men stood mesmerised, having never imagined, much less witnessed, anything like it in their lives. A deckhand explained to the men that they were in fact fish. Not birds, or bird-fishes. A Yorkshireman, who'd been as confused as anyone else but said nothing, now spoke up, "Birds my arse. Of course they're fish, anyone could see that." To guffaws of laughter, someone came back at him, "And you knew all along, Yorkie. But you didn't think to tell us." "Oh aye, common as starlings up North, they are," laughed Yorkie. John heard little of this banter, for the first in a long time he was thinking of Annahilt, "I wish some of the lads were here to see this. I really do. They'll never believe me when I tell them about it."

At 2:00pm on Saturday 25, the ship entered the harbour at Aden. At 4:00 pm the next day, on Sunday 26, after having taken fresh supplies of water and coal on board, it sailed away again. The temperature had risen higher than ever, and the men were glad to set sail. Happy to feel a sea breeze on their faces again, even if it was a hot one. The next day a dolphin was spotted. It seemed to be deliberately keeping pace with the ship, grinning up at and putting on a gymnastic display for its audience. Occasionally it would signal to them with blasts of its blowhole. The dolphin caused nearly as much of a stir as the flying fish had done.

The men of the 46th were enjoying their cruise on the *Oriental*. However, those who were starting to think that a sailor's life mightn't be so bad after all were about to get a rude awakening. The day after the sighting of the dolphin, a wind began to pick up, and before very long the ship was starting to roll. The wind kept getting stronger, and by around 3:30am the next morning it was at gale force. The ship was rolling as if about to capsize when above the noise of the storm there came the unmistakable sound of tearing fabric. One of the main sails had been torn to ribbons. If the ship had been rolling before it was nothing to how it behaved after losing the sail. It bucked and tossed, jumped from side to side, and appeared at times to leap clear of the ocean before re-entering with an almighty crash. Every so often it would almost stand upright on its nose. All the while there was the noise of crockery smashing, furniture being tossed about, sailors yelling orders and updates to one another, and a constant cursing and shouting from the men of the 46th. The soldiers, many of them by now violently seasick, were hanging on like grim death to whatever fixed part of the ship they could lay their hands on. This lasted for hours before the storm began gradually to abate, though not before it had torn another, thankfully less important, sail to shreds. As soon as it was possible, the sailors began to do running repairs to their vessel. The soldiers had always considered themselves a notch or two above sailors on an imagined hierarchical tree of servicemen. But after the storm, the 46th looked upon their seafaring companions with a profound sense of respect. Any thoughts of joining them had been forever banished from their minds.

After the storm had abated, a few days passed without incident, as things returned to normal. Grimly so. At 7:00am one morning two soldiers were brought on deck to be flogged. The first was to receive 25 lashes for sleeping on sentry duty (presumably not during the storm) and the second 50 lashes for striking a sergeant. After the commanding officer had completed the formalities of reading out the charges and the punishments, each man in his turn was taken to a metal grating that had been stood upright and fixed solid for the purpose. His shirt was removed and, with face pressed up against the grating and arms stretched out directly above him, his wrists were tied tight to it. He was then whipped across the back with a cat o' nine tails (a whip comprising nine strands with knots on the end of each strand) whatever number of times his sentence specified. Every soldier, and most of the sailors, had been assembled to witness the floggings, to serve both as a deterrent to themselves and as a humiliation to the prisoners (although one would imagine humiliation was the least of a prisoner's concerns at the time).

First up was the sentry who had been caught sleeping on duty a few nights previously. Although "caught" is hardly the apt term for what happened, as it tends to suggest that someone sneaked up on him while he was having a quiet doze. In fact a patrolling sergeant couldn't have avoided, even if he had wanted to, the loud and unmistakable sound of snoring coming from somewhere to the front of the ship. Upon investigating he came upon the sentry lying flat on his back on the deck, dead to the world.

The men, soldiers and sailors alike, always had a deal of sympathy for a man about to be flogged. But at the same time they were used to witnessing - and for some of them, undergoing - this form of punishment, so it didn't in the least bit horrify them. It was accepted as an integral part of their lives. To a degree, they even saw and agreed with the necessity for it. On the sentry, for instance, a man might say, "the movement of the boat probably rocked the lad to sleep. And no wonder, standing there for hours on end staring out into the dark, not knowing what he was looking for", and in the next breath declare, "he's lucky, though, that this isn't wartime, or he'd have been hanged for it. Falling asleep when you're supposed to be standing guard? Men have been hanged for less".

It was clear from the lack of any scarring on the sentry's back that he hadn't been flogged before, at least not seriously.

A tall sergeant stepped forward flexed himself a little and, upon receiving a nod from the officer, began to deliver the punishment. At the landing of the first stroke across his shoulder blades, the young man, despite his best efforts, let out a muffled yelp. It was the same with the second, third and fourth. Then his back started to go numb, and he was able, jaw clenched tightly, to stay silent as the remaining strokes were delivered. By the tenth, spots of blood were visible on his back. And before the end it was coloured entirely red, as the blood flowed freely. The sergeant began to tire at about the fifteenth stroke, and from that point on his face gradually took on a crimson colour, as if in sympathy with the sentry's back. By contrast, the sentry, who had been ashen-faced from the moment he had put foot on the deck, was even more so by the time he was helped off it.

When the sergeant had finished his work, he stepped back, and looked over at the officer. Who in turn nodded to a sailor who was standing by with a bucket of seawater. The sailor doused the sentry's back with the water and retreated. While the salt in the seawater made the wounds sting excruciatingly, it also helped cauterise them and went some way towards guarding against infection. The officer thanked the sergeant while the sentry was being cut loose from the grating. He then addressed the sentry, saying in long-winded fashion what amounted to, "now let that be a lesson to you". Then the sentry was half-carried away to be looked at by the regiment's doctor.

It was then the turn of the soldier, an old sweat, who had struck a sergeant. He was to receive 50 strokes, twice that of the sentry. Again the officer read out the charge and the designated punishment. When he had finished, Fletcher, for that was the prisoner's name, looked directly at him and said only one word, "Sir", then turned on his heel and walked to the grating. When Fletcher's shirt was removed it was clear that the flogging wouldn't be a new experience to him. His back was a mass of scars, testament to previous encounters with the cat o' nine tails. Two sergeants would administer the punishment, each delivering 25 lashes.

The officer would not have been aware of what had led to Fletcher striking the sergeant, not that it would have mattered if he had. There was no such thing as extenuating circumstances for an offence such as this (not that the army was big on extenuating circumstances, for any offence). Or perhaps the officer did have an inkling, for the victim of the assault had not been chosen to help administer the punishment. Or maybe the sergeant's omission was just an attempt to signal to Fletcher something along the lines of, "now don't take this personally, but rules are rules". The men had a great deal of sympathy for Fletcher. Not only was he well-liked, but he had proven himself many times to be "solid as they come in a tussle". To be fair, there were no strong feelings about Sergeant Johnston, the NCO he had assaulted. Johnson was neither liked nor disliked any more or less than were the other NCOs. But he and Fletcher detested one another, and had done since their first meeting. Nowadays, it would be described as a "clash of personalities". The problem was that one of them had stripes and the other didn't. And the first could never resist taking advantage of his rank to pick on the second.

On the day of the assault, Johnston had been throwing jibes at Fletcher on and off all day, trying to provoke a reaction: mocking his accent, making sneering comments about where he was from (Newcastle, as it happens), and how lazy he was. To Fletcher's credit, he reacted to none of this. So Johnston upped the ante. He started making accusations about Fletcher's family. Still no reaction. Finally, Johnston made a particularly crude remark about his mother. Fletcher, who was bent over fixing some kit at the time, stood up, turned around and, with a roundhouse swing, caught Johnston full on the point of his chin. Sergeant Johnston was knocked cold. Fond and all as they were of Fletcher, the men's sympathy only went so far in his case, too. "It's his temper that always does for Fletch. He has to learn to bite his tongue and walk away. Else he's going to get himself into real bother one of these days."

As arranged, the two sergeants delivered their 25 strokes each. Throughout it all, Fletch never uttered so much as a groan. At the finish, he had been bloodied but he was not bowed. After the officer had delivered his little speech, Fletch responded with, "Sir," and walked towards the hatchway, unaided. He stumbled and began to succumb to his injuries only when he got beyond sight of those assembled on the deck. But he had already made his point. Throughout the flogging, Sergeant Johnston had stood looking on. As it proceeded he became visibly less and less comfortable. After the last lash was delivered, he gave such a sigh of relief, it was as though it was for him that the torture was over. Johnston never again said so much as a word out of place to Fletcher.

Two days after the floggings, came another unsavoury incident, though this time one that directly impacted everyone on board. To supply enough water for a ship, seawater had to be boiled in a large metal container. The steam from the boiling water would then pass along a copper or iron pipe and condense as clean (or at least cleaner) drinking water in another large tank. One morning, two rats were found drowned and stewed in a condensing tank that the entire ship was reliant upon for water. The errant rats had, presumably, been scalded by the steam and fallen dead or dying into the tank. There they remained, for goodness knows how long, until discovered. The men were appalled, but there was nothing that could be done except remove the rodents and continue with the process of desalination. To empty the tank completely and start refilling it again from scratch, would have taken so long that most of those on board would have died of thirst before the process was complete. When word of the "water rats" reached John, he almost vomited in disgust. "Dirty wee bastards," he exclaimed, "I can't stand them. I really can't." His appreciation of the rodent had apparently been left behind in Crimea. Eight days after the incident with the rats, 23 days after leaving Suez, and a full 39 days since they departed Corfu, the men of the 46th bade farewell to the *Oriental. 1)* They had finally landed in India, at Karachi (now in Pakistan), in the early hours of the morning of Sunday, October 11, 1858.

1) Overland to India - By Donkey: A Journey, From the personal dairy of Lance Sergeant Samuel Robert Taylor, 46th (South Devon) Regiment, Journal of the Society for Army Historical Research Vol. 78, No. 314 (Summer 2000), pp. 102-114 (13 pages) Published by: Society for Army Historical Research, https://www.jstor.org/stable/44230240; Also, JA's record of service via Army Attestation Papers; and the official records of the 46th (South Devonshire) Regiment of Foot

The introduction of railways supposedly benefitted the Indian people

Chapter 4

India

The India that Britain captured and controlled was much larger than the modern-day state of the same name. British India, or the British Raj as it later became known, covered the entire Indian sub-continent and included, along with a few other states and regions, today's Pakistan, Bangladesh, Sri Lanka (previously Ceylon), and Myanmar (previously Burma). Some regions enjoyed a measure of autonomy, either as British protectorates or under the administration of a local prince, but all were ruled by Britain.

The British East India Company functioned as the sovereign power in India, on behalf of the British government, until 1858. At which point, its powers were transferred to the British crown. In 1876, Queen Victoria was declared Empress of India by the British government. At its height, the population of British India was in the region of 400 million people.

The official British presence in India began in 1612 with the establishment by the British East India Company of a factory at Surat, in the west of the sub-continent. By 1800, the East India Company controlled its own army of 200,000 soldiers, which was more than twice the membership of the official British Army at the time. *(1)* The British presence ended with India gaining its independence in 1947. For most of the period between 1612 and 1947, India was known as the "Jewel in the Crown" of British imperialism. And with good reason. It has been estimated that between 1765 and 1938 the British exchequer benefitted from India to the tune of £33.5 trillion. *(2)*

So it was indeed a jewel, but one bought and maintained at the expense and misery of the Indian people. Not just through the exploitation of themselves and their country's resources, but by the wars, poverty, famines, uprisings, and outbreaks of disease that were exacerbated by, or came as a direct or indirect result of, British rule. This is aside from the innumerable humiliations and degradations that countless millions of Indian subjects had to endure as an everyday part of their lives. Thomas Munro, a Scottish soldier and colonial administrator who was appointed Governor of Madras in 1819, summarised the British attitude to the Indian people in a highly-critical 1820s report to the directors of the British East India Company: "… none has treated them [the Indian people] with so much scorn as we, none has stigmatised the whole people as unworthy of respect, as incapable of honesty, and as fit to be employed only where we cannot do without them." *(3)*

It has been said in their favour that the British brought the railways to India, which is true. However, leaving aside that railways would surely have arrived there at some point anyway, it was not as though their introduction was done with the interests of the indigenous peoples in mind. The railways allowed Britain to draw raw materials from every corner of India and ship them home to be processed in British factories. Some of the processed goods would then be shipped back to India and, via the same rail system, transported to every part of the sub-continent to be sold to local people at extortionate prices. Whether deliberate or not, this kept local populations in perpetual impoverishment.

Colonisers seldom spoke of what they were taking from a colonised people, but concentrated instead on what they, supposedly, were bringing to them. This was no accident. Nor was it deliberate duplicitousness, or at least not entirely. The British did indeed believe that what they were bringing to India (and to their many other colonies) was something of unquantifiable value. They were bringing them civilisation. And there was no nation on earth more qualified to deliver civilisation than themselves. They felt they were doing the locals a favour by travelling there and teaching them British values. Whether the locals appreciated it or not was neither here nor there, it was the Christian duty of Britain to civilise them. That a few individuals and Britain as a whole profited enormously in the process was a mere by-product of their munificence. A sign from God, even, that they were implementing "His Plan". Of course there was something about the Indian people that could never be brought into line with Britishness, the colour of their skin. So it followed that Indians and other people of colour could be civilised only up to a point, but never entirely. They were, by God's design, a lesser people.

A fundamental part of God's plan was the spreading of His word. And to do that, local religions had to be challenged and defeated. Not that there was anything particularly novel in this. Colonisers from time immemorial have sought to impose their own religious beliefs and mores on native peoples. Europeans, including the British, were no different. So it was, "with a rifle in one hand and a Bible in the other" that the British sought to bring the Indian people "to salvation". Swarms of Christian proselytisers, working alongside the army and British administrators, were ruthless in their fervour, wholly convinced that they were doing God's work. Their attitudes, methods and approach, never mind their incessant attacks upon the cultures and devoutly held religious beliefs of their targets, were among the underlying causes of the Indian Rebellion of 1857. (And the United Irishmen Rebellion of 1798.)

History has it that the rebellion began with the refusal of a detachment of Indian Muslim and Hindu troops to bite open cartridges for a new Lee Enfield rifle, fearing that the cartridges had been greased with pork or beef fat (the first abhorrent to Muslims and the second to Hindus). However, this is only part of the story. The cartridge issue was viewed by the Indian soldiers as a final bridge too far in the ongoing British contempt for their religions. Indeed, so incensed were the soldiers they promptly killed their British officers and marched on Delhi. Soon fighting between Indian and British soldiers had spread across northern India (with some outbreaks of anti-British violence also occurred in the south at Tamil Nadu, near the Himalayas). By the time the British regained control a year later, at least 100,000 Indian soldiers had been killed. Estimates are that a further one million civilians were also killed in unprovoked attacks by British forces.

After the recapture of Delhi, a quote from an unnamed British officer of the East India Company was published in the *Bombay Telegraph* and reproduced in the British press. It gave some idea of the scale of the retaliation against civilians: *"All the city's people found within the walls of the city of Delhi when our troops entered were bayoneted on the spot, and the number was considerable, as you may suppose, when I tell you that in some houses forty and fifty people were hiding. These were not mutineers but residents of the city, who trusted to our well-known mild rule for pardon. I am glad to say they were disappointed."*

The officer was under the command of an Irishman, Brigadier General John Nicholson, who was born in Dublin but lived in Lisburn from a very young age, and educated at the Royal School Dungannon. A statue of Nicholson stands in the grounds of the Royal School Dungannon and another in the centre of Lisburn. It has been claimed that Nicholson and his men executed thousands of rebel soldiers and civilians on the march to Delhi. *(4)* He had a long, well-documented history of murderous violence against Indians that he deemed to have transgressed in some way. On one occasion he cut the head off an Indian bandit and displayed it on his desk as a warning to others. *(5)* Nicholson's history and the above quote from one of his officers give weight to the charge laid against him of indulging in a killing spree on the march to Delhi.

Far from the British people being horrified at reports of this and numerous other atrocities being committed in their name, they were delighted to hear of them. Newspapers, politicians, church leaders, and most anyone else who had a public platform, were all of the same opinion: no amount of retaliation was severe enough punishment for the treachery and ingratitude of the Indians. It was as though the Indian people had risen up and bitten the hand that fed them, rather than the other way around. Even the author, Charles Dickens, who did so much to highlight the plight of the poor, oppressed and exploited in his homeland, was moved to write in October 1857: *"I wish I were commander-in-chief in India ... that I should do my utmost to exterminate the race." (6)*

The Indian writer and historian, Amaresh Misrahas, has claimed that post-1858 the British launched a 10-year campaign of retaliatory attacks on civilians, from which the death toll could be as high as 10 million men, women, and children. *(7)* It is estimated that at least 15 major famines occurred during the time of British rule in India. There has been speculation that the worst of these, The Great Indian Famine of 1876-1878, may have been allowed happen as punishment for the uprising of 1857. However, it is probably more accurate to say that Britain always put its own economic interests above the lives of the indigenous peoples of its colonies. And this was the case in India, just as it had been in Ireland during *its* Great Famine. The payment of taxes and the delivery of foodstuffs and other products for export were demanded of the people by the colonial power, regardless of circumstances. In 1876 regular exports of grain by British government representatives in India continued despite the famine. Indeed, a record 320,000 tonnes of wheat, alone, was sent to England that year. *(8)* Between starvation and associated outbreaks of cholera, dysentery and other diseases the famine eventually claimed around 10 million lives. There were so many dead that not all of the bodies could be buried or cremated.

It should be stated, though not by way of an excuse but for context, that Britain was not the only coloniser of the time. All of the larger nations of Europe, and even some of the smaller ones, were engaged in empire building. Britain just happened to be better at it than the rest. Moreover, based on their own experiences, the people of Congo, Burundi, Rwanda and many other places might well claim that Britain was far from the worst in terms of its treatment of native populations. But to engage in such comparisons not only runs the risk of appearing to minimise or make excuses for the wholly inexcusable, it entirely misses the point. The point being that a coloniser, who had no right to be there in the first place, and exercised absolute power over indigenous peoples.

Karachi

Karachi is nowadays the capital of Pakistan's Sindh Province, and home to more than 16 million people. It is the largest and most populous city in Pakistan, and the country's premier industrial and finance centre. However, in 1858, when John Adams arrived there with the 46th, Karachi's population numbered just 57,000. But even then the city was growing rapidly, owing mainly to its well-placed location on the edge of the Arabian Sea.

Because of where it sat, the British constructed a new port and installed a railway at Karachi, and it wasn't long before it became the major transportation hub for India. This led to the city's population continuing to grow rapidly in numbers for almost a century. Then it exploded. After the partition of India in 1947, hundreds of thousands of Muslims fled to Karachi to escape the religious and ethnic violence that engulfed India upon, and for some years after, partition. By May 1948, it was home to 470,000 refugees. And another 100,000 refugees would arrive annually until 1952. *(9)*

John was to stay in Karachi for only a little over four months, but it deserves mentioning in detail here, for it was there that he fell in love with India. He would have struggled to put his finger on specifically why. Its confusion of colours, smells (particularly of spices), and the constant busyness of the place enthralled him. And he was equally enthralled by India's profusion of strange creatures, both wild and domesticated. Birds of every colour, shape and size seemed to fill the air and walk upon the ground. At first light one morning, he left the barracks to investigate the source of a horrible squawking that had awakened him, and there standing before him on the lawn was the most wondrous bird he had ever seen. A peacock. "So beautiful. So very beautiful," he muttered to himself, completely awestruck. The first time he saw an elephant being worked by its handler his eyes nearly popped out of his head. The size of the beast - like a small cottage, he thought - and its strength, yet it was so gentle and obedient.

The army barracks at Karachi were by far the best he had ever stayed in. *(10)* Spacious, airy, and kept spotlessly clean by local workers. Local staff also cooked and did laundry for the men. John soon got to know many of the workers and found them to be industrious, friendly, and welcoming people. Always helpful, and with a lovely sense of humour. They too, like the Turkish soldiers in Crimea, put him in mind of people back home. They would take a little while to assess someone before opening up fully to them.

There is a well-worn cliche that says people are all fundamentally the same, no matter where in the world they are from. John would never have heard this saying, but he learned the truth of it on his travels. It first struck him during his army training. As soon as he got to know his fellow trainees, he began to recognise the same character traits amongst them as the people he had grown up with. Some stranger from

Birmingham may not have looked or sounded in the least like Big Billy from just over the fields at Annahilt, but in most other respects he was his double. Big Billy was fundamentally a decent man, but there were also a few - thankfully only a few - who in the same way were the double of Wee Sleekit Skelton from Comber, whom you couldn't trust as far as you could throw him. And, just as with the neighbours back home, the great majority of his fellow trainees fell somewhere between these two extremes. It was the same when he went to Crimea and mixed with new colleagues there. And again in Corfu and India. Crucially, what soon struck him was that it was not only his fellow British soldiers he experienced this with. The same was true of the Turks he met in Crimea, though neither he nor they spoke a word of one another's language, and with the native peoples of Corfu and of India. No matter where he went, he kept meeting people that he felt he had met before – except, of course, he knew that he hadn't *actually* met them before. He wouldn't have put it this way, but he became convinced that skin colour, language, religious belief, and any number of other cultural differences, were really only a veneer. Beneath this, he decided, there are only a relatively tiny number of character types.

Karachi's population is nowadays 97 per cent Muslim. But in 1858 it was much more religiously diverse, home to sizeable Christian, Hindu, Sikh, Zoroastrian and other minority religious communities (the large-scale population shifts from 1947 onwards went both ways). Most of these religions were represented amongst the workers at the army barracks.

John himself was far from religious, although he liked the idea that if there was a Heaven the option was there for him to make himself eligible for admission before he died. He was not, however, "a believer" in any true sense of the term. But he did know quite a bit about the basic tenets of Christianity (which is a different thing altogether from being a true believer). He could hardly not have known about his religion, having spent a sizeable portion of every Sunday until young adulthood sitting in a church pew (like almost everyone else in Ireland and Britain at the time). Having only ever been acquainted with the narrow diversity of his own country, he was intrigued to learn that there were so many other religions. Wanting to know more, he would occasionally chat with workers at the barracks about their beliefs, but soon became hopelessly lost in the complexity of most of them, "so many different gods in charge of so many different things". Not so with Islam.

It was striking to him how much in common Islam appeared to have with Christianity. The same God, the same prophets, the same stories about the lives of the prophets, a shared belief in the Virgin birth of Jesus, the miracles that Jesus performed, the crucifixion and the rising of Jesus to Heaven, and so on. Even Allah, the Islamic name for God, isn't a name as such. Translated literally from the Arabic, it simply means "the God". The only major points of difference, or so it seemed to John, is that Muslims do not believe Jesus was God, or even a Son of God, but a prophet. And that he wasn't the last prophet, which was Mohammed. According to Islam, both Mohammed and Jesus were ordinary men whom God chose to work through, such as in the miracles that *He* performed *through* Jesus. *(11)*

John Adams probably learned more about Islam in 1858 than the vast majority of non-Muslim people know today. Though it would appear he was not the only European to learn about Islam during their time in India. On April 20, 1874, The Englishman's Overland Mail carried the following report: *"The Northern India News has heard that two Europeans employed on the Sind, Danjib and Delhi railway turned Muhammadans at Lahor last week, the ceremony being performed at a mosque near the Lahore fort."* The overall tone of the report probably says more about the two newspapers than it does about the European converts. During his interactions John would occasionally be confronted by some glassy-eyed fanatic from one or other religion who was more interested in lecturing than listening. This was no novelty to him. He had come across plenty of the same sort back home. As his mother would often describe them, "The type of people more interested in twisting religion to suit themselves than twisting themselves to suit religion."

Sarah

On February 19, 1859, John left Karachi for the punjabi city of Multan (now part of Pakistan) some 884 km (550 miles) to the east. His was one of four companies of the 46th that travelled ahead to Multan, while the same number of companies remained behind at Karachi until they could be relieved by another regiment. The advance party, as it were, boarded the steamship *Havelock* and travelled along the Indus River to Multan. *(12)*

Today, Multan is a much smaller city than Karachi, with a population in the region of two million people to Karachi's 16 million. In 1859 however, Multan was the larger of the two, its citizens then numbering about 65,000 to Karachi's 57,000. In 1848 it had been the scene of the Multan Revolt, when local Sikhs murdered two emissaries of the British who were in the city to officially anoint a replacement to the Sikh leader who was considered a despot by many of the local inhabitants. This led to widespread conflict across the Multan region, between those loyal to the leader and those who preferred his replacement. The British, intent on revenge for the murder of their emissaries, were now doubly determined that the current leader should go. They had their way, and more besides. What became known as the Multan Revolt led to the Second Anglo-Sikh War, from which the British emerged victorious. Defeat in the war led to the fall of the Sikh empire in 1849. During the Multan Revolt, Sikh rebels and their soon-to-be-replaced leader took refuge in Multan city, to which the British laid siege and finally captured. The scars of the British bombardment of Multan were still visible when the men of the 46th arrived there some 10 years later. The men had become acclimatised to excessive heat during their stay in Corfu, the journey to India, and the few months they had spent in Karachi. But nothing could have prepared them for Multan. When they arrived the average daily temperature was 40C. Over the next few months it would rise steadily to reach its annual peak of around 52C during June and July. The monsoon rains between June and September alleviated the heat a little, though they markedly raised the risk of infection from any number of insect- and water-borne diseases. The area was and remains prone to dust storms during the summer months.

The accommodation at Multan was not nearly as good, or in nearly as good a state, as it had been at Karachi. Between that and the weather, many men began to fall ill. After the other four companies arrived in April, at least 80 men of the 46th were laid low at any given time. *(13)* New huts were in the process of being built when the 46th arrived, each to hold 70 men, and these were soon finished. But while they would have been considered fine, excellent even, if located somewhere in Kent, they were not designed with Multan's climate in mind. Built with brick walls, and tiled roofs around steel frames the huts proved very hot and uncomfortable for those that had to live in them. But none of this bothered John too much during 1859. He had other things on his mind. As had been his custom in Karachi, he began to make friends with the Indian staff working at the Multan barracks.

One day, on his way to chat with an old carpenter he had become acquainted with, he happened to pass close by a group of local women putting laundry out to dry. One of them caught his eye, just at the moment that he had caught hers. Each smiled in embarrassment, then looked away. The next day he found an excuse to pass them by again. Upon spotting him coming the women began laughing, throwing glances in his direction, and nudging and making comments to the woman John had locked eyes with the previous day. They were obviously teasing her about him. The young woman herself giggled with embarrassment, shaking her head while making "don't be ridiculous" noises, and looking everywhere but in his direction. This sort of thing continued over the next few weeks: him walking by, trying to act as though he just happened to be passing on his way to somewhere else, the women laughing and teasing, and her studiously avoiding looking at him. Finally he plucked up the courage to stop and approach the women. "Hi, I'm John," he said, and stuck out his hand to the nearest one to him, "How are you doing?" Not the most original or romantic first words ever spoken, but he had broken the ice and that was all that mattered. He shook hands with each of the women in turn, and learned their names. He proffered his hand to the young woman, and this excited more giggles from her friends. But she grasped it without hesitation and looked directly into his eyes, "Thank you. I am Sarah. I am pleased to meet you, sir." "Oh for goodness sake, please don't call me that. Call me John," he replied, genuinely appalled at the notion of anyone, particularly this young woman, calling him "sir". "Okay, John," said Sarah, and giggled.

It wasn't long before John and Sarah were an item, spending almost every minute of their spare time together. They would walk and talk, often while exploring the town, with her explaining its recent history and introducing him to the local customs and food. He generally liked the food, though found some of it a little too spiced for his taste.

John would tell Sarah about Ireland, the greenness of the land and the friendliness of the people. And, hypocritically, would sometimes even wax lyrical about the beauty of the flax when in full bloom. The winters in Ireland, he explained, "Can be very cold at times, but all you need do is stick on a few extra bits of clothes." She was shocked to hear about Ireland's great famine, "People starve to death in your country too?", she responded in amazement.

Sarah was small and dainty, a little under five feet tall, and of the quiet, unobtrusive sort. Deferential too, which John would try to encourage her not to be. But that was how she was. Underneath it all, though, Sarah was steely and determined and, a bit like John himself: hard to turn once she had set her mind on something. They spent the summer and autumn of 1859 falling deeper and deeper in love. Then December brought with it the news they had both been dreading.

When the British soldier in India was not fighting, drilling, parading, doing guard or sentry duty, or carrying out maintenance work, he was invariably marching off to do the same things somewhere else on the sub-continent. And so it was in December of 1859 that the 46th learned they would be leaving Multan in February of the following year, to take up post at Jalandhar (now spelt Jullundur) some 450km (or 280 miles) away. John and Sarah couldn't bear to imagine not seeing one another again. So they did what each of them had been hoping to do all along, and decided to marry.

As tended to be the case with women in those days, and particularly women of Sarah's background, little if anything was documented about her. But this much is known for certain: genetic tests on descendants of hers [including this author] show that her forebears came from every compass point of the Indian sub-continent. Punjabi genes from Northern India, Gujarati from Western India, Bengali from Eastern India, and Sri Lankan Tamil from Southern India. These, as well as some broadly east Asian genes, remain present in her descendants. Sarah, or one or both of her parents, had at some point been "Christianised", hence her first name.

Sometime between December 1859 and February 1860, John and Sarah were wed. *(14)* At the time, British soldiers had to obtain permission from their commanding officer to marry. But it was not worth the while of lower ranks bothering to apply, as only about six per cent of applicants were ever given official permission to marry, and those were invariably officers. And only then if the intended bride was British or European. Most men who were of a mind to marry a local woman just went ahead and did it anyway. Nor did they suffer any overt sanctions for doing so. Army commanders were not naive enough to think it was possible to locate thousands of men in numerous countries around the globe without them seeking the company of women and occassionally falling in love and wanting to marry.

One of many reasons the commanders sanctioned so few marriages was they didn't want the responsibility, particularly the financial responsibility, of providing for the wives and children of soldiers. The wife of a sanctioned marriage was entitled to half the daily food ration of her husband, to provide for herself and their children. Not very much, it's true. But the wife of an unsanctioned marriage received nothing. A sanctioned couple would be eligible for married quarters if or when these were available, whereas an unsanctioned couple would never be granted quarters of their own. And if every marriage was automatically sanctioned it would inevitably give rise to major logistical as well as financial problems when a regiment was posted back Britain.

But the major reason so few marriages were sanctioned, far above all others and dictated by the British government and strictly adhered to by every branch of British officialdom, was that Indian wives and mixed-race children of soldiers should not be entitled to come to Britain. The fear, to put it bluntly, was that the supposed purity of the

British race would risk contamination if such people were entitled to return home with their soldier husband and father. The British army rules in respect of its men marrying local women were not only applicable in India, but in every other British colony with a non-white population. (This attitude developed from a fundamentalist religious fervour that began to spread throughout Britain in the early to mid-1800s.) Upon marriage, whether sanctioned or not, a wife would move into the barracks where her husband and up to 70 of his comrades lived. A blanket would be strung along either side of the couple's bed to allow for some privacy. If children came along, they would share the same space as their parents. The wife would cook and clean for her husband. And often, to earn extra money, for some of his unmarried colleagues as well.

There was no obvious hierarchy amongst the sanctioned and unsanctioned wives, they regarded and treated one another as equals. And indeed, in everyday interactions, were treated and viewed as equals by men and NCOs alike. The everyday difference for the unsanctioned wife and her children was that the barracks and self-sufficiency were as good as it would ever get. And living with a constant dread of the day when her husband had to say goodbye to India, for he would be waving goodbye to her and children as well. (It hardly needs saying that the vast majority of men had no intention of ever marrying their sweetheart, much less bring her and any children they had back to Britain. When the time came, they would leave for home with hardly a backward glance.) *(15)*

On February 20, 1860, the 46th set off from Multan to march the 450km (or 280 miles) to Jullundur. Trailing along behind were the wives and children, Sarah among them. The families formed only one small part of an extensive caravan of "camp followers". The rest was made up of people eager to look after the needs of the soldiers - at a price of course. The camp followers sold goods and services such as food, clothing, liquor, cooking, laundering, nursing, and sexual favours. Before the 46th left Multan they had received a ringing endorsement from the commanding officer there, an aptly-named Brigadier Colin Troup, which was carried in the *Army and Navy Gazette* of March 10, 1860. Troup was about to retire from the army and wanted to place on record his high estimation of the 46th. He had served for 39 years in India and "had to deal with many different regiments during that time", but of all those he had dealings with over the years, "none has given me more universal satisfaction than the 46th", he declared. The brigadier felt assured that the "uniform good conduct of the 46th will at all times elicit the admiration and goodwill of whatever officer may have the honour of commanding it". Troup told the men that he "parts with them with the deepest regret, and wishes each and all of them health, happiness and prosperity wherever they may go". John had chosen his regiment well that day at Newry. Or rather, Sergeant Dobson had chosen well for him.

Jullundur

The army had picked the best time of year to travel to Jullundur. That is not to say it was a particularly good time to set out on a 280 mile (450km) march, just a lot better than it could have been. During February and March, average daily temperatures in Jullundur were between 22C and 26C. From April to June they would steadily rise to reach a daily average of between 35C and 45C. The march was not in fact terribly taxing on the men. The heavier equipment was carried on donkeys, and most of the rest by locals hired for that purpose. The soldiers would stop at villages along the way to stock up on fresh water and buy meat, fruit and vegetables, much to the consternation of the camp followers who dealt in these items. In the early evenings, a halt would be called and tents pitched. Men would be joined by their wives and children, if they had any, and food would be prepared. The family would spend the night together, then they would separate again the next morning. John and Sarah spent every night of the journey together, of course. She was particularly good at sourcing and buying extra food for the two of them, which is hardly surprising. Being local, she knew what to look for and where to find it. And for the same reason, vendors knew that, unlike the Europeans, she was not open to exploitation. There was hardly a night passed when she didn't arrive at the campsite with some tasty treat for their supper.

John and Sarah enjoyed the march, feeling they had more freedom and privacy than at the barracks at Multan. Nor was it as if the soldiers were moving at any great pace, covering on average about 13 miles a day. This gave John plenty of time to look around him; to see "the real India", as he thought of it, beyond the hustle-and-bustle of its big towns and cities. Like a wandering tourist he would gaze wide-eyed at the countryside, the people, and the wildlife as he walked along. Men and boys working the fields with their oxen, or pulling and wrestling a plough through the soil themselves. Villages full of laughing children, who would rush excitedly to greet them. And shy mothers and older sisters, who would look away anxiously to avoid meeting a soldier's eye.

The wildlife was beautifully kaleidoscopic in all of its colourful unpredictability. One day they spotted a snake at least four metres long, its girth comparable in circumference to that of a small child's waist. The porters were afraid to go near it, and nor did the snake seem particularly comfortable with suddenly being the subject of a human audience. As it slid slowly away, John marvelled at how closely the markings on its skin matched the foliage into which it was disappearing. They stopped for a full day, a Sunday, at Lahore, more than three-quarters of the way to Jullundur. On another day they couldn't proceed at all because of heavy rains.

One evening Sarah raised something with John that had been nibbling at the back of her mind for some time. She hadn't wanted to mention it before, partly because she was afraid of leading him to doubt the reasons she had married him, but mainly through fear of what the answer might be. They were lying in bed, and John was describing Annahilt and telling her what it was like growing up there, when suddenly Sarah turned to him and asked, "What will happen when you have to leave here to go home?" "What do you mean?" replied John. There was no turning back for Sarah, even if she had wanted to, "What will happen to me when you have to leave India?" John raised himself up on one elbow, and looked directly at her, "You're my wife, Sarah, and I love you. When I have to leave India, you'll be coming with me." He said it with such obvious sincerity, she didn't have to ask if he meant it. "I won't pretend to know yet how I'm going to manage it. But trust me, I'll find a way to make it happen. One thing's for certain, I'll not be leaving India without you," he declared. Sarah hugged him tight and kissed him, as happiness and relief flooded through her. "I love you too, John. With all my heart."

On March 20, 1860, exactly one calendar month after they left Multan, the 46th arrived at Jullundur. They moved into barracks that, if they weren't already close to perfect, they soon would be. In a few years time, 1864, a report by a commission specially appointed to *Inquire into the Sanitary State of the Army in India* would be made public. When the 46th moved into Jullundur the members of this commission were still touring British military establishments in India, gathering evidence. It's clear that Jullundur was well prepared to receive them. According to their report, the cantonment (military barracks) at Jullundur was in excellent condition. There was accommodation for 1,200 European and 3,000 "native" troops, with 16 to 24 men to each well-aired spacious room. The commissioners rated everything at Jullundur, from the married quarters through to the water supply, the lavatories, the hospitals, the latrines, the bedding and the cooking, either good or excellent. There were, according to the commissioners, ball courts and skittle alleys, a regimental school, and a library with a "well-lighted" reading room. Their one slight criticism concerned drainage, and the fact that filth being taken away in carts was being allowed sink into the ground. Though they countered this by describing the overall sanitary state of the barracks as "Most healthy". And while they found the men to be "temperate; with no confirmed drunkards" they suggested that the sale of spirits should be abolished and replaced by "beer, tea, coffee, etc" as spirits were "injurious to health and discipline". Modern-day holiday camps have had worse reviews than that given to Jullundur barracks by the commission. One has to wonder how far in advance the barracks commanders knew of an upcoming visit by the commissioners. Regardless of this, if the review was anywhere close to accurate, the men must have been delighted with their new accommodation. Although the vast majority of them were probably unaware that there was "a library with a well-lighted reading room" never mind them ever having had a chance to use it.

Bella

Time passed slowly and easily at Jullundur. The barracks provided excellent accommodation and leisure facilities for the men. Their duties were easy, if monotonous. But no more so than anywhere else they had been. Since in the recent past there had been some incidents in the area linked to the 1857 Uprising, the troops did not entirely drop their guard. But the locals were friendly, and the troops never encountered any trouble.

For John and Sarah, life at Jullundur was much like it would be for a married couple in Ireland or Britain. He would leave for work first thing in the morning, and return home in the evening, when they would share a meal that she had prepared. Her days were spent cooking, cleaning, and doing laundry in the company of the other women.

A year almost to the day after they arrived at Jullundur, Sarah had news for John. He had begun to suspect that something was on her mind. Nothing bad, he thought, because she didn't seem overly worried, just a little distracted. He asked her a couple of times, "Are you okay?", and she assured him she was. So he decided to leave it at that. If it was something important, she'd tell him in her own good time. It was typical of a man that the obvious never crossed his mind. One evening after supper, as they were strolling around the camp, she took his hand and announced, "I think I'm pregnant." He was stunned, "You're pregnant? Are you sure?" His reaction worried her. Staccato like, she replied, "I'm not certain. But nearly certain. It's early yet. Are you okay with it?" "Okay with it? Okay with it? I'm delighted with it. Absolutely delighted, Sarah," he yelled as he grabbed her, and held her in a tight hug. "There's not a happier man on earth at this minute," he whispered to her. She cautioned him that it was still very early, so nothing could be taken for granted just yet. "But what do you think? Are you nearly certain? Or are you certain but you don't want to count your chickens just yet?" he asked, sounding like a particularly annoying child. She had no idea what chickens had to do with anything, but she knew what he meant. "The second one," laughed Sarah. John was ecstatic. Laughing and giggling, he grabbed her by the hands, and danced around her. He had never felt so happy in his life. And neither had she.

One would think that John, having been raised in a rural setting and been around pregnancies and births all of his life, might have been relaxed about Sarah's prenatal period. But not a bit of it. This wasn't some pregnant heifer or ewe that he was keeping an eye on for a neighbour, but his wife and his baby. He was a bundle of nerves from start to finish. Over the months that followed, he was attentive to the point of being a nuisance. "Are you okay?", "How are you feeling today?", "Do you think you should be lifting that?" "Here, let me do it." As her bump got larger, he would sometimes run his hand over it in a loving fashion. She liked him doing that. When the bump got bigger still, and she would sometimes move around with a hand placed on one hip, he started with the over-attentiveness, again. "Is your back sore again?", "Is it supposed to be as sore as that?", "Lie down here and I'll rub it for you." She liked him rubbing her back.

As the approximate time of the birth drew nearer, she learned not to wince or, in particular, let out so much as a tiny groan, if John was around, or he would launch into a panic of questions. "Has it started?", "Do you want me to get one of the women, for you?", "Should we make our way over to the hospital?", "Are you sure it hasn't started yet?".

In the early afternoon of November 03, 1861, John was standing chatting to some local men while on guard duty at the entrance to the barracks, when a sergeant approached him and, with a smile on his face, said, "You should report to the hospital, Adams. I believe you're needed there." For a split second John wondered why on earth he was needed at the hospital, then he was off running, a large grin plastered across his face. He knew everything must be all right, or the sergeant wouldn't have been smiling.

When he burst into the hospital room, Sarah was sitting up in bed, as calm as you like, suckling their new-born baby. With a wide grin she said, "Come and meet your daughter, John." He thought her the most beautiful child he had ever seen. As he gently stroked her cheek with his index finger, she seemed to look up at him and smile. "Thank you, so much," he said to Sarah. He leaned down and kissed her on the forehead, "You've made me the happiest man in the world. I love you.," then shifting his gaze from Sarah to the baby, and back again, "I love you both. My two beautiful girls."

Sarah had felt the first pangs of labour in the early hours of that morning, but hadn't said anything to John. "I didn't want to worry you," she explained. It was more like she didn't want to have to deal with a panicking husband while coping with the pains of labour, and trying to judge when it was time to call one of the other women and make her way over to the hospital. She had finally gone to the hospital at around 10:00am, and the baby was born shortly after noon. It was an easy birth, without the slightest complication. "Girls are always easier than boys," according to the soldier's wife who had helped her. The baby was christened Bella at Jullundur by army chaplain, James Sharpe, on November 10, 1861. *(16)* Sarah and John had been anxious for a month or so prior to Bella's birth, and became even more so after she was born. The 46th had received orders in October to take up post at Cawnpore, some 500 miles (805km) away. They would be leaving Jullundur to march to Cawnpore on November 30, a mere 27 days after Bella's birth.

1) The Encyclopaedia Britannica, https://www.britannica.com/story/5-fast-facts-about-the-east-india-company
2) Essay by economist, Professor Utsa Patnaik, Agrarian and Other Histories: Essays for Binay Bhushan Chaudhuri, Shubhra Chakrabarti and Utsa Patnaik (eds) (New Delhi: Tulika Books, 2017)
3) The Dynamics of Global Dominance: European Overseas Empires, 1415 - 1980, by Professor David B. Abernethy, Yale University Press 2002
4) Ruling the World: Freedom, Civilisation and Liberalism in the Nineteenth Century British Empire, by Alan Lester, Kate Boehme, and Peter Mitchell, Cambridge University Press December 2020
5) Cult of a Dark Hero: Nicholson of Delhi, by Stuart Flinders, Published online I B Taurus 2019, Bloomsbury Publications 2002
6) From a 4 October 1857 letter from Dickens to Baroness Burdett-Coutts. Originally from LETTERS Of CHARLES DICKENS to The BARONESS BURDETT-COUTTS etc, Published by E. P. Dutton & Co., Inc, New York, 1932, and quoted by innumerable sources since
7) War of Civilisations: India AD 1857, Vols 1 and 2 by Amaresh Misra (Delhi: Rupa, (2007)
8) Export of food grains, a potent cause of famines in India between 1860 and 1900 by A C Sahu, proceedings of the Indian History Congress, vol. 39, Indian History Congress, 1978, http://www.jstor.org/stable/44139428.
9) Karachi: Disorder and the Struggle for the City, by Laurent Gayer, Publishers New Delhi: Hurst & Co. Publishers (2014)

10) *From an 1864 report by a commission appointed by the British to Inquire into the Sanitary State of the Army in India (Note: This is the source for other descriptions of barracks, accommodation etc.) Wellcome Collection https://wellcomecollection.org/works/sw53b769/items*
11) *The Islamic Jesus, by Mustafa Akyol, Published by St. Martin's Press, 175 Fifth Avenue, New York, N.Y. 10010 (2017)*
12) *From JA's Attestation papers and British army records (Note: One or both of these sources for all other movements/relocations) https://www.fold3.com*
13) *From the Army and Navy Gazette of June 11, 1859 www.search.findmypast.co.uk*
14) *To date, a record of the marriage of John and Sarah is yet to be recovered (if one still exists). But they are invariably described as husband and wife in subsequent church and even army records (see citations for mentions of family births, and deaths) leaving no doubt that a marriage did indeed take place.*
15) *The King's Shilling: Life in Army Barracks 1855-1871, by Hilary Greenwood, November 2011, http://www.littlehamptonfort.co.uk/wp-content/uploads/2014/03/Kings-Shilling-3.pdf; Britain's Forgotten Wars: Colonial Campaigns of the 19th Century, by Ian Heron, Published by The History Press (2016) 16) Baptismal record for Bella from Jullundur, https://www.fold3.com*

Other Sources: *The Anarchy: The Relentless Rise of the East India Company, by William Dalrymple, Bloomsbury Publishing (2020); A History of India, by John Keay, Harper Collins*

Above: *Brigadier General, John Nicholson. Born in Dublin and raised in Lisburn he was a hero to many. But to most Indians he was "The Butcher of Delhi", and was labelled an "imperial psychopath" by the historian, William Dalrymple.*

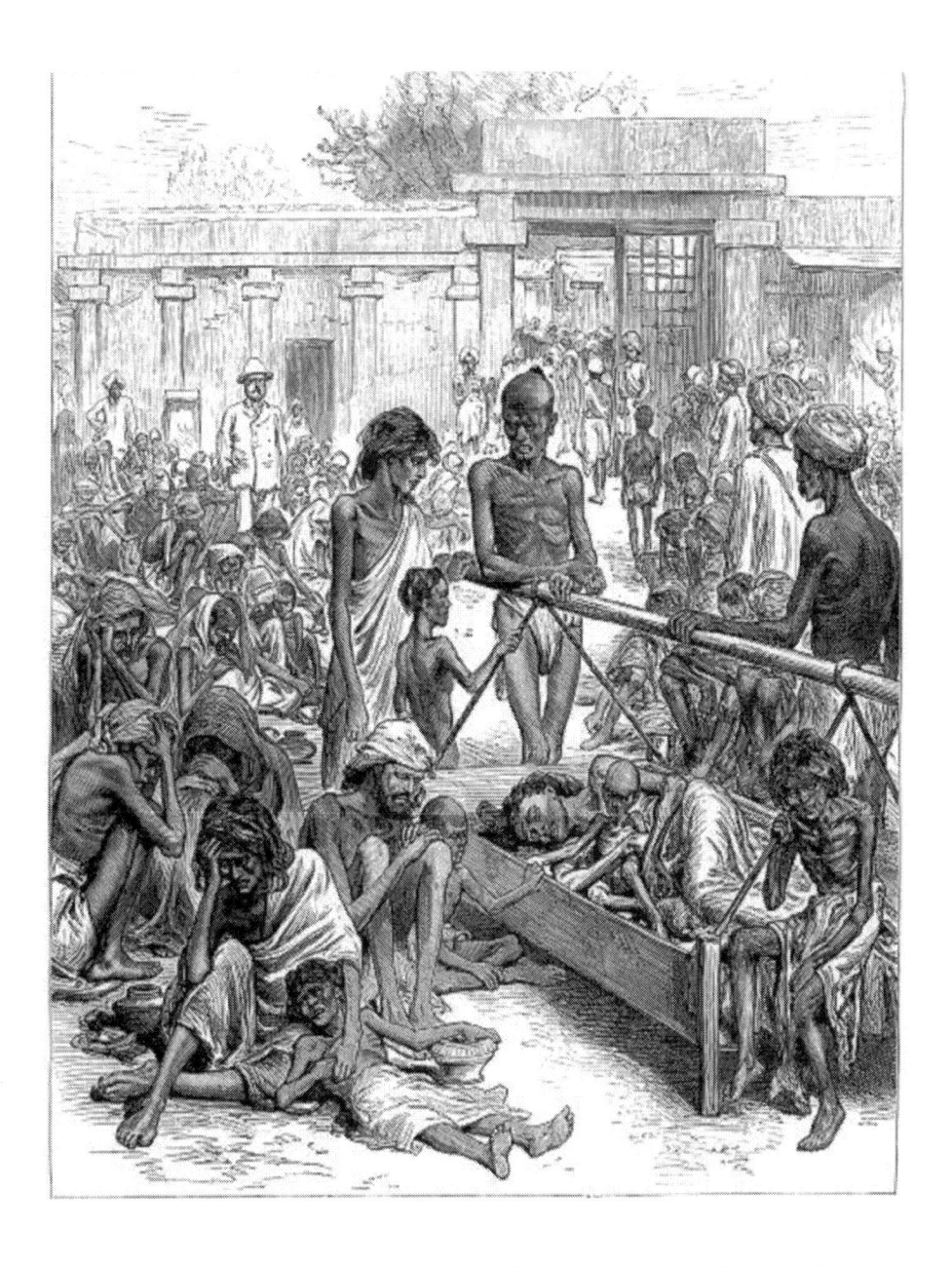

The Great Famine of India was one of at least 15 major famines that occurred there during British rule. (Note how fit and healthy the British gentleman in the background appears to be.)

Chapter 5

Cawnpore

On November 30, John and Sarah set off with the 46th to walk the 500 miles to Cawnpore. Sarah carrying their new-born child, Bella.

It was clear before even the first day was out that this trek was going to be nothing like the relatively relaxed jaunt to Jullundur they had undertaken some 20 months earlier. This time they were to travel almost twice the distance, so the officers were constantly pushing the men to cover at least 20 miles a day. There were to be no rest days or stoppages of any kind unless it was absolutely impossible to keep moving forward. Not even Christmas Day was exempt from this, when the 46th would march for 14 miles. It was hotter, with daily temperatures between 37c and 40c, and many of the roads were in such poor condition they often amounted to little more than dusty tracks. Fruit, vegetables and other foods, such as they had enjoyed on the march to Jullundur, were much scarcer and harder to find, and for that reason often so expensive they were beyond buying.

By the middle of the second week, Sarah was deeply worried about Bella. Previously a bight-eyed inquisitive little thing, she had become listless and wouldn't suckle as often or for as long as before. At first Sarah thought it might be the heat, and Bella would brighten up again once she had become acclimatised to it. But as the days passed there appeared to be no signs of improvement. If anything she seemed to have deteriorated a little. As if lacking in energy, she had taken to whimpering rather than crying. Existing on little beyond a shared army ration, Sarah and John were themselves struggling for nutrition. This was doubly hard on Sarah, for she had to carry Bella mile after mile in the heat. Her milk began to dry up. She tried feeding Bella sweet potato boiled to mush and mixed with a little bread, but the child would spit most of it out. Although the women of the 46th rallied round Sarah and did what little they could to help, most were mothers too and struggling to keep their own offspring nourished. Luckily a woman from amongst the camp followers had not long since given birth herself, and - for a fee, of course - agreed to suckle Bella occassionally.

Day-after-day the marching continued. Each night Sarah and John would cuddle Bella and hold her tight, as though love alone could help sustain their daughter. And possibly it did. For as December gave way to January, Bella began to rally a little. Each day, as they inched closer to Cawnpore, the communities they passed through had a little more food for sale. Sarah was able to buy or, most often, beg what it took to sustain them. Her milk began to flow again. The 46th reached

Cawnpore on January 13, 1862. Bella, Sarah and John had made it, but only just. As the weeks passed at Cawnpore, and they were able to rest, eat and recover, Bella gradually got stronger. Their fears lifted, Sarah and John began to relax.

In February came news from England that fuelled an excited round of gossip among the men, plus a good deal of hilarity and any number of bad jokes. It came in the form of reports of a junior officer of the 46th having appeared in civil court on a charge of attempted murder. A Lieutenant William McRea of the regiment had appeared before the Thames Police Court the previous October, charged with attempting to murder one George Pavey, a cook and steward on the ship, *Northumberland*. McRea was on his way home to England from Madras. Pavey showed the court a large scar on his forehead, a result of McRea attacking him for no reason with a large heavy metal instrument called a maul. Pavey said that if he hadn't managed to partially block the blow with his hand, he would surely have been killed. As it was, his hand was disabled, he lost a large amount of blood from his head wound, and for many days "his life was despaired of". The maul was produced in court, still heavily bloodstained. McRea had apparently followed Pavey to the ship's galley (cookhouse), and as the cook was leaving the galley the defendant had, for no reason, struck him "a swinging blow" with the maul. Pavey called out for assistance, and McRea was overpowered and secured. Speaking in McRea's defence, a lawyer told the court that the defendant was on his way home after being invalided out of India, and suggested that he may be suffering from insanity (a reasonable enough suggestion, seeing as that was the reason McRea was discharged by the 46th). The magistrate, displaying all the empathy he could muster, retorted "I do not sit here to try questions of sanity" and promptly remitted the case to the Central Criminal Court. *(1)*

"I hear that as he was hitting yer man, McRea was shouting: 'I told you I wanted my eggs poached not boiled'", John declared to some of his mates, mimicking a faux posh accent. "Did he?" exclaimed Shorty, the failed jockey, with eyes and mouth wide open in shock. "No he did not, ye wee eejit," laughed John, equally as incredulously. Multiple variations on "Christ, if he'd do that to a top cook on a ship, what would he not do to the people cooking here," did the rounds among the men. As did quips along the lines of, "My woman can't so much as boil an egg. She doesn't know how lucky she is that it was me and not McRae she fell in with." For months afterwards, the men would gently mock their womenfolk about the meals they set down to them, with cracks such as, "I'll eat it, but I'll bet you McRea wouldn't."

In March, Sarah told John that she was pregnant again. Though both of them were pleased, neither felt they could afford to be ecstatic. They had come too close to learning how tenuous life can be for a child to feel they could afford to take anything for granted. And they were to have that lesson driven home, in the most painful fashion.

Bella never fully recovered from the march to Cawnpore. After they arrived at the camp she had begun to feed normally again and even gained a little weight. She seemed as bright and alert and interested in the world around her as any baby of her age should be. But she was very prone to illness. Most particularly to fevers. Hardly a week went by, it seemed, that Bella was not drenched in sweat and suffering a high temperature. It all took its toll on her. In the early hours of the morning of July 01 Sarah awoke and knew instinctively that something was wrong. She reached out to Bella, and the child was icy cold. Their darling daughter was dead.

Sarah would remember very little of the next few days. John's abiding memory was of the spine-chilling scream from his wife that had wakened him. Bella was laid to rest on July 03 at Cawnpore camp, with Army Chaplain J A Stamper officiating. Over the following month, the Rev. Stamper would lay another three infants of the 46th to rest at Cawnpore. John and Sarah were never to know it, but their child was wrongly named in the registration of her death and burial. Christened Bella, the registration of her death has her as "Isabella". An understandable human error, given the number of burials of infants at the time. Perhaps someone filling out the register had asked, "What was the name of the Adams child we laid to rest in July?" And the answer came, "It's Bella," and this was misheard as "Isabella". Or perhaps someone just assumed that Bella was short for Isabella. Whatever the reason, it seems a cruel twist to an already tragic tale that the child's name couldn't even be recorded properly at the end of her all-too-short life. *(2)*

Sarah had always been a bubbly, outgoing, and essentially positive person. But after Bella died she sank into a deep depression. She became quiet and listless and uninterested in much of what was going on around her. She missed her child terribly. But worse than that, she blamed herself for Bella's passing. She felt like a failure. Felt as if she had failed as a mother. Ironically almost, at the same time as she was convincing herself of this, Sarah was forcing herself to keep eating for the sake of their unborn child.

John was as distraught as his wife at the loss of Bella, but, as can be the way with men, he kept it largely hidden. He was quieter than usual, and slower to smile and engage in idle chat with his colleagues. But those were the only outward signs of his agony. In truth, John was deeply distracted, and by more than the death of Bella. He was worried about Sarah and their unborn child. She was a small woman, diminutive even, and pregnancy showed on her. But even allowing for that, she looked enormous. Her belly was far bigger than it had been at a similar stage of her pregnancy with Bella. Either their dates were wildly wrong, which was hardly likely given that Sarah had fallen pregnant so soon after Bella's birth, or something else was. By September, Sarah could hardly move around, she was so big.

In the late evening of October 01, Sarah went into labour. At 1:30am the following morning, October 02 1862, a baby boy was born. An hour later, another baby boy followed. Sarah had given birth to twins. But all was not well. It was clear they were born prematurely, and would do well to survive. While an orderly rushed off to fetch the chaplain, John sat with Sarah, his hand upon her shoulder, as she tried to suckle their sons. The weaker of the boys was christened first. They named him Samuel. The other little boy was christened William. *(3)*

Samuel died within hours of being born. He was buried the next day in Cawnpore camp, beside his sister, following a funeral service once again conducted by the Rev J. A. Stamper. The men of the 46th, of all religions and none, trooped into the Anglican church at Cawnpore to pay their respects and express their condolences to one of their own and his wife. John recited the Lord's Prayer at the service, which Sarah of course was not fit to attend. He also read some passages from the Bible that had been chosen for him by Rev Hamper. It was the first anyone in the 46th realised that John could read and, presumably, write. His mother had taught him from an early age to do both. No one had ever asked him, and he had never volunteered the information. (Something else the old man on the cart outside Dromore had advised him, "If you can read and write, tell no one. Or you'll be spending every spare minute writing letters home for your pals".)

For a short while it seemed as though William might pull through. But sadly he too passed away, on October 24, three weeks to the day after his birth. He was buried the next day alongside his siblings, the ritual conducted this time by S. B. Burrell. John wasn't asked to contribute to the service this time. One glance at him and Sarah, wrapped in one another's arms, tears streaming down their faces, was enough to show that he wasn't in a fit state to do anything. *(4)*

There is a modern-day assumption about times past that goes along the lines of "people in those days were so accustomed to losing loved ones that they didn't feel it as keenly as we would today". A natural extension of this view (widely held, though seldom openly expressed) is that people who nowadays live in countries with exceptionally high mortality rates - from illnesses, disease, conflict, natural disasters, and so on - have likewise become hardened and somewhat immune to the loss of their loved ones. Only those who have never been to such a country and witnessed the anguish of a just-bereaved parent, partner, offspring, or sibling could ever believe this to be true. No matter where they are situated and no matter the tragedies that might befall them, people do not in any way become immune to losing loved ones. They do not "learn to live with it" as some people like to imagine. They carry on *despite* their loss, because they have no other option. And that's exactly how it was for "people in those days". And that's how it was for Sarah and John. She slowly regained her strength, if not her zest, and she and John gradually carried on despite their loss.

For many a couple, each wrestling with seemingly unrelenting personal pain, the loss of three babies over a matter of only a few months might have driven them apart. But it brought Sarah and John even closer together. It was as though each felt that the other was all they had left in the world. And that they must make the most of their partner while they were still able to, for there was no way of knowing when their togetherness might end. They had seldom argued before, but after the loss of their three children they never exchanged cross words again.

John did all he could to ensure that they would not be parted if he could possibly help it. He had been waiting for a solution to come to him on how he would manage to bring Sarah home to Ireland, but by November 1864 he was still waiting. A six-month short-term posting to Shahjahanpur, during which time Sarah and the other wives remained at Cawnpore, gave him more thinking time. Eleven years and six months more, to be exact. There were only six months remaining of his initial 10 years service in the army, so he signed on again. He was happy to do so. He loved Sarah, and there was no way on earth he was going to leave her.

Sarah rallied after the deaths of the children, but she was never quite the same again. Aside from when she was alone with John, she became a far less open and demonstrative person. It was as though she was always carrying a terrible weight inside herself. And that indeed was the case. Sarah hated Cawnpore for what it had taken from her. But at the same time she dreaded leaving the place, because she felt she would be abandoning her babies. Still, life was such in the army that she knew someday they must leave, and it was only a matter of time before they received orders to do so.

In December of 1864, rumours began to circulate to the effect that the 36th regiment based at Lucknow was in "poor health" and would soon be sent to relieve the 46th, who would essentially change places with them and move to Lucknow. The rumour had in fact been picked up from newspaper reports and proved to be accurate. (Indian and British newspapers of the time reported extensively on military matters. Even down to the minutiae of troop movements.) *(5)* The following month, January 1865, the 46th were ordered to prepare to take up post at Lucknow, and in early April they left Cawnpore. Lucknow was a mere 57 miles (91km) away, and they completed the march in just five days. Before they left Cawnpore, Sarah and John visited the grave of Bella, Samuel and William for one last time. They laid a few flowers that Sarah had picked, and, through floods of tears, told their children that they loved them, and would see them again one day. After a little while they said their goodbyes and left. They were wracked with guilt. Not only were they leaving the children, but it felt as though they were on their way to replacing them, as Sarah was pregnant again. It was wholly irrational for them to feel guilty about the pregnancy, but when have emotions ever been rational.

Lucknow

Only a few years earlier, in 1857, Lucknow had been one of the major centres of the Indian Uprising. Rebels had seized control of the entire Uttar Pradesh state, of which Lucknow was and remains the capital. It took the British a full 18 months to reconquer the region. During that period, the British army garrison was besieged by rebel forces during what became known as the Siege of Lucknow (there were actually two sieges at Lucknow during the period of the uprising. The first lasted for 87 days, and the second for a further 61 days).

The city was settled and quiet when the 46th arrived to take up post. But the uprising was fresh in the minds of soldiers and public alike, so no one was totally relaxed. For the soldiers of the 46th, Lucknow represented a change in location, but not much in the way of a change to their everyday routine. They drilled, trained, carried out guard and sentry duties, and engaged in the general upkeep of the barracks, just as they had done at every other place they had been stationed.

For Sarah and John, those first few months at Lucknow were both an exciting and a fearful time. As the weeks went by, and her baby bump grew larger and the expected time of her delivery grew ever-nearer, she and John became more frightened. Neither voiced it to the other, but both were thinking the same thing, "I can't imagine being able to cope if anything happens to this baby." It need hardly be said that neither felt they had the luxury, or the audacity as they would have put it, to hope for a boy or a girl. They never even thought about it. A healthy baby, of whatever sex, was all they wished for. That would be more than enough for them.

Late in the evening of August 20, 1865 Sarah went into labour, and in the early hours of the next morning she and John were delivered of a fourth child. It was a baby boy, whose sustained yowling upon entering the world was enough to tell them that he was healthy and full of life. Relief and joy flooded through them both. But most particularly Sarah who, though wary of taking anything for granted, felt some of the inner pain and unfair guilt she had heaped upon herself lift at the moment of his birth. Still cautious, not wanting to tempt fate, they waited a full seven weeks before they had their son christened.

Finally, on October 14, William Adams, son of Sarah and John, was baptised at All Saints Garrison Church in Lucknow, with the ceremony performed by the Rev Milward R Burge. They decided to name him William. *(6)* That one of the twins had also been called William would suggest that this was the name of John's father, but as yet there is no evidence to confirm or refute this.

William was indeed a healthy thriving boy, not least because of the love and attention his mother showered upon him. If he so much as squeaked she would be checking that he was all right, and generally fussing around him. Or as John laughingly and approvingly put it, "She'll not let a fly land near that child." There's nothing Sarah liked better than showing William off to the other women. Her friends knew what she had gone through, some quite literally as they had lost children themselves, and were delighted for her. "Oh, he's lovely, Sarah. Such a handsome little chap," was the universal refrain. Not that a person will ever say otherwise when viewing another's baby. But in this case it was true; William was a beautiful child. He was born with a mop of dark brown, almost black, hair. (Which prompted John to remark in amazement, "My God, this child is half-reared.") His hair was perfectly matched by large brown eyes and a dark skin colour. In a perfect example of someone stating the blindingly obvious, John told Sarah, "I think he looks more like you than me." "No, no, he has your chin and your lovely smile," she countered. "I'm not complaining," said John, "I'm delighted. Sure doesn't that mean he's going to be the most handsome young fella that God ever put breath into."

Though their marriage had not been officially recognised by the army, and never would be, John managed to get married quarters for himself and his family at Lucknow. In truth, this wasn't difficult to achieve. Lucknow, as the capital city of Uttar Pradesh state, was the centre for all government related administrative, political, and social activity. This status was reflected in the British army barracks in the city. Large, spacious, and much of it extensively refurbished or newly-built after the uprising in 1857, the barracks had more than enough in the way of accommodation for the regiments based there. Which included a surplus of married quarters. John, and a few other old sweats from the 46th who were married to local women, had only to apply and were almost immediately granted leave to move into quarters of their own. The bungalow that John and Sarah were given was fifth in a row of 10 identical structures. Each consisted of a sitting room, a kitchen, and two bedrooms, and had a privy in the backyard. A table, two chairs, two beds, two sets of blankets, and a tiny amount of crockery and cutlery came with the house. All of which, down to the last spoon, had to be returned in immaculate condition whenever the couple moved out again. Otherwise, the soldier would have the cost of any damage, breakages, or missing items deducted from his wages. It was all very basic, at least by today's standards, but felt like the height of luxury in comparison to what Sarah and John had been used to. At last the little family had somewhere they could call their own, and most especially had the long wished-for privacy that came with it.

From the outset, Sarah would chat to William in both her native tongue, Urdu, and English. The former particularly when they were at home alone. So the child grew up equally comfortable with either language. He would express himself in whichever took his fancy at any given time, and sometimes in a mixture of the two. John took no notice of this at the start, thinking the child was just babbling away in baby-talk. But as William got older, and began to speak more coherently, he became concerned. He might be leaving for work, and William would run to say goodbye with, "Khodafez, Papa." Or when John came home, he would greet him with, "Khush Aamdeed, Papa. I have missed you." Though he had never bothered to learn the language, John was familiar with spoken Urdu, but not the baby-talk version of it.

One evening, while William was sleeping, he raised the matter with Sarah, "It might be nothing. And I don't want to worry you, for what would I know. But is William struggling a wee bit with the talking?" "No he is not," said Sarah defensively. Then, at a loss for what the problem could be, "Why do you ask?" Halfway through John explaining as best he could what was bothering him, Sarah collapsed in fits of laughter. With tears running down her cheeks, she managed to say, "He is speaking Urdu to you, my darling husband." John could do nothing but laugh himself, "God, aren't I the right eejit." As he got older, William would learn to separate the two languages. And, depending upon the background of the person he was speaking to, would converse exclusively in one or the other. Though when he and his mother were alone together, they would always chat in a mixture of the two.

There was an important interruption to William's early childhood while he was learning to express himself. Three weeks short of his second birthday, on August 01, 1867, he was joined by a baby brother. Sarah had of course been worried during the pregnancy. But not nearly as much as she had been when carrying William. It was the same for John, except he had found something else to worry about. After finding out that Sarah was pregnant, he was wracked with guilt when he thought about William. "My God," he wondered, "How's the wee fella going to feel when we land in here with another child?" And, as if a parent has the capacity to love only one child at a time, he could not imagine loving another youngster to the same extent that he loved William. So of course he began to worry too on behalf of the child yet to be born. Sarah, being a woman and a mother (never mind having a larger dollop of plain common-sense than her husband), had no such concerns. She instinctively knew that a parent's love is not a zero-sum game between his or her children. John eventually settled down without feeling the need to confide in Sarah.

It was a soldier mate of his from Dublin, a father of four, who set his mind at rest. "Don't talk bollox," was Big Seamie's considered reply to John's long-winded and convoluted explanation of how he was feeling. Then Seamie, in his usual succinct manner, and speaking from personal experience of his own children, elaborated a little on why John was talking "bollox", "You'll see what I mean as soon as the child is born." In later years, John liked to say, "Never ask a man from Belfast or Dublin a straight question unless you're prepared to take a straight answer back. For there's no back-doors in them people. None at all." No doubt Big Seamie was one of those John had in mind.

Irishmen of every persuasion and from all parts of the island tended to stick together in the British army, not in any overtly clannish or exclusive manner, they just had a natural commonality and were comfortable in one another's company. It was much the same with the Scottish, the Welsh, and men from the same geographical regions of England.

John had a particular fondness for Kerry people, and would often say, "I've never met a man from Kerry that I didn't like. You couldn't meet more decent people." And in the next breath, "But I'll never visit the place. For as sure as anything I'd run across the biggest waster in the county, and that would ruin it for me." There was a blanket disparagement of Kerry people, widespread at the time, that suggested they weren't terribly bright (it had about as much basis in fact as another old saw about all Scots being miserly). John would laugh if someone so much as hinted at the Kerry disparagement in his presence, "Oh aye, stupid as a fox they are. The same people could buy and sell you if they took a notion."

The new baby was baptised on August 11, 1867 at All Saints Garrison Church in Lucknow, this time the ceremony was performed by Chaplain Henry Murray. He was christened John Henry, and would be known by all as "Jack". *(7)* As with William, Jack had brown eyes and a mop of dark brown hair, and was of dark complexion. He was slightly smaller than his older brother had been at birth, but only just. And certainly not to the extent that would cause any worry.

As for John, just as Big Seamie had predicted, he fell in love with Jack the moment he saw him. And nor need he have worried in the slightest about William's reaction. The older child was delighted to have a younger brother, and fussed over him almost as much as Sarah did. And so the happy little family settled down again to a contented life, with Sarah heaping love and attention on the boys and their father. As with William, she chatted to Jack in both English and Urdu almost from the moment he was born. And William did the same, of course. John revelled in his role as father, husband and provider. He would sometimes think, "I should really be pinching myself to check that all of this is real."

While chatting one day with some of her neighbours, Sarah heard of the latest rumour that was doing the rounds. And it frightened her. According to the rumour (which had again originated in the press) the 46th was going to be recalled to England - the military authorities having decided that the regiment had more than served its time in India. *(8)* Sarah's first thought was the same as that of the other wives of unsanctioned marriages, "What will happen to me and the children?" As soon as John got home she raised it with him. "Don't worry," he said, "I have it nearly sorted. I'm in the middle of transferring to another regiment." He laughed, "You didn't think I was going to head off and leave you and the boys here, did you?" That was in April, 1868. A couple of months later, on July 01, John transferred to the 55th (Westmoreland) Regiment. He was given a new regimental number, 1477. *(9)*

It was far from uncommon for a British soldier in India to transfer to another regiment upon learning that his own was about to be recalled to Britain. Invariably it would be those who had spent a long period in the country, and had put down roots. Such as having married a local woman with whom he had children, as was the case with John. The practice of regimental transfers suited all sides. Most obviously the soldier and his wife and children, but also the regiment he was leaving. The expense of shipping him home would be avoided, and he could easily be replaced by recruitment back in Britain. Critically, the regiment would not have to deal with the inevitable discontentment in the ranks caused by a number of the soldiers being separated from their families.

For its part, the soldier's new regiment would be recruiting a man with years of experience in India. A quick check with his current regiment would ensure that he was of acceptable character, and would not prove to be more trouble than he was worth. As far as the 55th was concerned, John Adams suited them perfectly. As well as his years of experience, he had seen combat in Crimea and was the holder of four Good Conduct Badges. To put this in perspective, a survey between 1870 and 1898 found that no more than five per cent of soldiers in the entire British Army were the holders of three Good Conduct Badges, never mind four. *(10)* Besides, the 55th were based in Lucknow at the same time as the 46th, and its NCOs and men, and possibly some of its officers, would have known John well. And this worked both ways. John knew the 55th well, and was aware that though he was leaving a highly respected regiment, the one he would be joining was at least as well thought of. A few months after John transferred, the 55th was inspected by a General Brooke Taylor, who found the regiment to be, "In admirable condition. Very strong in officers and exceedingly smart in its movements". *(11)* Shooting competitions were a big feature of the 55th during the regiment's time in Lucknow, and this was reflected in a *Times of India* report in September 1868 that commented on the "high percentage of marksmen" within its ranks. On October 01, the 46th left India for England. It was with genuine sadness that John said his goodbyes to many old friends and comrades, some of whom he had known since Crimea. But this was largely offset by the knowledge that he would not be travelling with them.

William and Jack were not aware of any changes, of course. They continued as usual to see their father off to work in the morning and greet him when he came home again in the evening. And between times they would enjoy life at home with their mother. Though sometimes the time spent with their mother was more enjoyable for

William than for Jack. They were both intelligent youngsters, but even from an early age it was clear that they had very different personalities. William was quieter and less demanding than Jack. He was also more amenable to discipline. As the boys got older, Sarah continued to spoil them with love and attention, but she was also determined to instil some discipline into them. This was relatively easy with William, who tended to put up token resistance to a demand then smile and accede to whatever his mother wanted. Not so with Jack, who would often dig his heels in and refuse to budge. William, it appeared, was all for making life as easy as possible. Whereas Jack's idea of an easy life was having things all his own way. But his mother never gave up. She too would dig her heels in until Jack did what he had been told.

Sarah was only too aware that this would be the easiest period of her boys' lives, whatever the future had in store for them. She had witnessed what it was like for someone to grow up as mixed-race - European and Indian - and knew the stigma attached to it. It meant not being fully accepted by either side. Many Indians, would refer to mixed-race people as "kutcha butcha", a term of disparagement that literally translates as "half-baked bread". To most Europeans they were just another two Indian boys, and therefore, by definition, inferior to themselves. Her boys were, to all but an unpractised eye, obviously of mixed-race. If they were to have any chance in life, they must learn what being kutcha butcha could mean for them. They also needed to have self-discipline and -control. Jack in particular had to learn to give a little more and not be so obstinate and, most especially, to control his temper.

John had got to know lots of men during his time in the army, and had been quite friendly with most of them. But such was the nature of army life, with people constantly coming and going, friends leaving and other men taking their places, he had learned to attach himself to very few colleagues. To think of them as not much more than close acquaintances. That changed when he joined the 55th and met Henry Pope (he had actually been christened Alfred Henry Pope, but seldom mentioned the "Alfred" part, even on official documentation). Henry was a likeable, generous and thoroughly decent man; fond of a laugh and a joke, often at his own expense. He and John hit it off immediately.

From Ilchester in Somerset, Henry was slightly taller than John at 5ft - 7ins, and a good deal younger. He was 30 when they met in 1868, and John was 38. He had joined the army in 1857, two years after John, and had spent all of his time in the "East Indies". Though Henry had never been to war, as such, he was nonetheless a very experienced soldier. And a very fine one, too. In fact, if John Adams was a very good soldier, Henry Pope was an exceptional one. He had served in the Somerset Militia before joining the 13th Light Infantry. He was promoted to corporal in the 13th in 1863, but relinquished his stripes that same year when, upon learning that his regiment was going to be posted back to England, he transferred to the 55th. Within four years of transferring, in 1867, he was again made a corporal. That same year he re-engaged for another 12 years, and was promoted to sergeant. *(12)*

In December 1867, Sergeant Henry Pope of the 55th was mentioned in the Kendal Times as a member of the "Sergeants Team" that came top in that year's inter-regimental shooting season in India.

It seems strange that John was never offered promotion, especially after it emerged that he could read and write. He was an experienced, dutiful soldier whose service record was exemplary. Maybe promotion was offered to him but he gracefully declined. He was well liked and respected by his colleagues and didn't want to jeopardise that by accepting a position where he would have to order them around and discipline them. He perhaps thought it impossible to be an NCO (Non-Commissioned Officer) and popular at the same time (although Sergeant Henry Pope was proof that it was indeed possible). Or maybe John just didn't want the extra responsibility. Still, it is difficult to imagine why a family man would, in effect, refuse the much-needed extra money and food allowances he would receive as an NCO. It seems more likely, though impossible to prove, that John was never offered promotion precisely *because* of his family. Were the military authorities concerned that promoting a soldier with an Indian wife and mixed-race children would send the wrong signal to other soldiers? Moreover, would the British Army's acceptance of John's marriage by such a promotion be legally tantamount to it accepting financial and other responsibilities to the family? In short, would a promotion entitle Sarah and the children to travel to the UK with John after his army service was done?

As alluded to above, Henry Pope somehow had the knack of being able to do his job extremely well, yet remain one of the lads at the same time. The only blot on his copybook came while he was still with the 13th Light Infantry. In 1861, he was court-martialled and sentenced to a month in prison for accusing an NCO of being drunk. The fact that he was made a corporal a mere two years later suggests that the army's attitude was, in effect, "The NCO may well have been drunk. But you shouldn't have said so."

John would often invite Henry back to his quarters, and soon he was a firm favourite of the boys. He was one of those adults that children take to immediately. The sort that can chatter away for ages to a child on his or her own level; who have a natural affinity with children. William and Jack loved it when Henry came to visit. He would wrestle and play with them, tease them, and was forever telling stories about Somerset. Henry was more than just a friend of John's. He was a much-loved friend of the whole family.

As with any group of people, and particularly those forced to live together, not everyone in the 55th always got along. In 1874, a Private James Lowe of the 55th went before a court-martial charged with assaulting a fellow soldier, John Allen, with a tent peg, causing him serious injury and endangering his life. Lowe was found not guilty of the charges, much to the disgust of his Commander-in-Chief, who made clear he disapproved of this finding because he thought there was enough evidence to convict. No doubt Lowe was delighted with the verdict. Whether he remained delighted for very long, is another matter altogether. It's hard to imagine the Commander didn't ensure that his life was made a living hell forever afterwards. *(13)* As always with the British army in India, John's regiment was soon on the move again, and the Adams family had to say farewell to Lucknow. This time they were off to Chakrata, close to the Indo-China border.

1) Grantham Journal, October 11, 1862, www.search.findmypast.co.uk
2) Church record of Bella's burial as described above. Reason for death, "dentitis", https://www.fold3.com
3) Church record of the baptisms of Samuel and William, https://www.fold3.com
4) Separate church records of the funeral services for Samuel and William, https://www.fold3.com
5) Madras Times, October 20 1864; Army and Navy Gazette, December 31, 1864 et al, www.search.findmypast.co.uk
6) Church record of William's baptismal service at All Saints Garrison Church in Lucknow on October 14 1865, https://www.fold3.com
7) Church record of the baptismal service for John Henry at All Saints Garrison Church in Lucknow on August 11, 1867 https://www.fold3.com
8) Times of India report of August 27, 1868, www.search.findmypast.co.uk
9) JA's Attestation papers, https://www.fold3.com
10) The Late Victorian Army, by E.M. Spiers, published by Manchester University Press (1992)
11) Report carried by The Army and Navy Gazette on October 03, 1868, www.search.findmypast.co.uk
12) From the British Army Attestation papers of Sergeant Alfred Henry Pope, https://www.fold3.com
13) Reported by the Englishman's Overland Mail on April 10, 1874, www.search.findmypast.co.uk

All Saints Church in Lucknow, where William and Jack were baptised

Chapter 6

Chakrata

On March 01, 1869, the 55th left Lucknow for Chakrata, 530 miles (850km) away. The men, not to mention the women and children, would no doubt have been happy that a large part of the journey was undertaken by rail. By April 01, they arrived at their destination. The men's mission was to refurbish, and largely rebuild, an army hill station there. The women and children of the regiment were moved temporarily to Sitapur until suitable accommodation could be built for them. That being the case, the men tackled the accommodation aspect with vigour, at least the family part of it, and their loved ones were able to join them within three weeks.

Sitting close to the foot of the Himalayas, Chakrata is world-renowned for its scenic beauty. The new station was situated on a plateau some 2,500m (8,000ft) above sea level, surrounded by forests and waterfalls and, not surprisingly, teemed with wildlife. And that's why the army chose it. It had been decided it would be much healthier for the troops if they were stationed on high ground, breathing fresh mountain air, above the illnesses and diseases that ran rampant at ground level.

The families of the 55th couldn't have chosen a better location themselves. Sarah and the boys loved Chakrata. It was like a holiday destination to them. (Not that any of them had ever heard of, never mind experienced, such a thing.) They would walk along the mountain paths, picking flowers and stopping to picnic on a few bits of food that they brought along with them. Though they never wandered too far from the camp. While William would skip alongside his mother, Jack was still only toddling, and had to carried much of the way. Besides which, within the beauty of the forests there lurked many dangers. While sitting outside the family's bungalow one evening, admiring the view with Sarah and the boys, with typical understatement, John looked around him and mumbled something like, "And I thought the Mournes were beautiful." Sarah had no idea what he was on about, but replied, "Yes," anyway. Before very long John would be reminded again of Ireland, but not of its scenery or beauty.

Not everyone was so happy at Chakrata, on July 01 an unnamed colour-sergeant of the 55th took his own life there. And, in the process, almost took the life of a colleague. The colour-sergeant had tied a stocking to the trigger of his rifle and wrapped the other end around his foot. He then placed the rifle against his forehead and pushed down with his foot. The bullet that killed him travelled onwards and narrowly missed the head of another soldier. *(1)* In another tragedy, one morning in 1871, while out riding in the hills around Chakrata, a Lieutenant of the 11th Hussars, W S Lillingston, fell to his death when the road he was on gave way under his horse. The road was skirted by a sheer precipice over which Lillingston and his horse fell more than 300m (1,000ft). Death was instantaneous. His remains - or probably more accurately, what remained of him - were collected the following day. *(2)*

It is sometimes said, usually by highly successful people, that "you make your own luck in this life". Which can often be true, but not always. Compare and contrast the fortunes of another officer of the 55th called Jobling, and those of an unnamed bandsman of the same regiment. In April 1874, Jobling went for a stroll outside his army base in India, and was promptly mauled by a tiger. He lay severely injured for many days, not expected to survive. But to everyone's amazement - not least his own, no doubt – he eventually made a full recovery. *(3)* Four years later, in England (Portsmouth), an unnamed regimental bandsman, who had been in India during Jobling's ordeal, reached down to stroke a cat and it reacted by scratching him on the hand. The poor man was dead from rabies within a matter of days. It seems you don't always "make your own luck". *(4)*

Throughout 1869, 1870, and into 1871, the men of the 55th worked to improve and extend the hill station at Chakrata. Building accommodation, a hospital, cook-houses, canteens, armouries, latrines, and so on. By early 1871 they had even built a theatre, and on May 18 staged their first productions, 'The Charcoal Burner", and a farce called, "Done Brown". *(5)*

By all accounts, of which there were many, the 55th did a marvellous job of rehabilitating and rebuilding Chakrata. If they could only have known what this would lead to, their work would surely not have been of such a high standard.

The Commander-in-Chief of the British Army in India, Lord Napier of Magdala, accompanied by a number of other lesser dignitaries and military commanders, visited the station in November 1870, and was deeply impressed by what the 55th were doing. He found the station to be, "The most charming place. Able to accommodate two to three full regiments." Other visiting dignitaries were similarly impressed. Viceroy Lord Mayo and a Major Bourke among them. In an address to the men of the 55th, Lord Mayo was fulsome in his praise, claiming that, "...while Chakrata remains a station, years, hereafter, the name of the 55th will remain unforgotten". Of course each high-profile visitor to Chakrata was accompanied by the press, and soon newspaper reports on what a magnificent job the "Troops on the Hills" were doing began circulating around the world. *(6)* When it came to building another hill station at Cherat, 660km from Chakrata, who else was going to be assigned to the job but the 55th. As a newspaper report put it in reference to Colonel Hume of the 55th, "...judging by the successful way he [Hume] laid out, and superintended, so to say, the new hill station of Chukrata (sic), a better selection for the appointment [to build Cherat] could not have been made" *(7)*

Depending on the status of the visitor, sometimes a photographer would accompany the journalists. Photographs were a new-fangled innovation, and the source of much amazed interest among the soldiers. One day John asked a photographer to take a picture of Sarah. The man obliged, and took a photo of her sitting on a swing. He wrote John's details in a notebook and promised to leave the photo for him to collect at Lucknow barracks. Six weeks later a Sergeant handed John a large envelope and said, "This was sent up to you from Lucknow." John opened it, and inside was the photo of Sarah on the swing.

Peshawar Fever?

By April, 1872 the 55th had left Chakrata and were stationed at Peshawar ("The City of Flowers") now in Pakistan. At the end of April, four companies, numbering 250 men, John Adams and Henry Pope among them, were sent from Peshawar to the hill sanatorium of Cherat, essentially to replicate the work they had done at Chakrata. The women and children remained behind.

Peshawar had something of a reputation. A bad one. Situated only 60-odd km from Chakrata, it might as well have been on another planet. The region was notorious for its lawlessness and tribal violence and commonly referred to as "the Badlands". In much later years, the city would be the destination for the world's first ever mass evacuation of civilians by aircraft. When, in December 1928, 600 people were airlifted from Kabul and deposited there. *(8)* Later still, it would be home to many hundreds of thousands of Afghan refugees fleeing the 1978 civil war in Afghanistan and, in 1979, the Russian invasion of the country. By 1980, approximately 100,000 Afghanistan refugees were entering Peshawar every month. In 2001, the leaders of the al-Qaeda organisation and their families, including Osama bin-Laden and his wives and children, would make their homes there. *(9)*

Sitting on low, flat ground and given to flooding, Peshawar plain in 1872 was alive with insects of every kind. As a consequence, its human inhabitants were prone to falling ill. Often going down with what had become known as Peshawar Fever (most likely a variant of malaria). The fever was described in the following terms by the Indian Statesman newspaper of July 10, 1872: "...the soldier who has contracted Peshawar Fever remains long afterwards so damaged in constitution as to absolutely require change of climate to Europe for the thorough restoration of his health. The physical deterioration is occasionally so marked that a regiment after it has been quartered for any time at Peshawar does not look like it has been composed of the same men...". Diarrhoea and dysentery were an everyday feature of life at the Peshawar army cantonment and, on average, there was a cholera outbreak every three years. And no wonder. The British army had uprooted a local Muslim community to the west of the city, and built their cantonment on top of a huge, centuries-old Muslim burial place. The water supply came from wells sunk down through the burial place to the water table below.*(10)*

At the outset, people were encouraged to boil water before consuming it. Whether they were told the precise reason for this precaution is unknown. With temperatures ranging between 36C and 48C for six months of the year, it is easy to imagine that thirsty people would often ignore the advice. Besides, given the constant turn-around in inhabitants at the cantonment, how long before people were unaware that such advice had ever been issued, never mind the reason for it?

All things considered, it is hard to imagine a more unhealthy place to set up home than Peshawar of the 1800s.

Sarah hated the place from the moment she laid eyes on it. "This is a bad place," she said to a friend. "I know, I hate it too. But it's probably because we're used to Chakrata," replied the friend, not unreasonably. "No, it's more than that. It's a bad place," said Sarah with emphasis, and a shiver. The boys missed Chakrata, too. And they missed their father. "He will be back soon, my loves. And we won't be here forever. We'll soon be moving to another place. You'll see," comforted their mother. They had grown so much over the past three years, she thought, and the mountain air has made them look so healthy. The mountain air and the sunshine had also deepened their skin colour. With their black hair and dark brown eyes, they could easily be mistaken for local children. Especially by a European.

This worried Sarah. It worried her a lot. John still had four years to serve in the army before his time was up. But then what? She had long ago stopped thinking about her own future, the future of her boys was all that concerned her now. Sarah would listen as they chatted to one another in accents that were a strange mix of Indian and Irish-English (of the guttural, northern Irish variety) with the hint of a semi-English accent on the occasional word. The last picked up, presumably, from spending so much time in the company of the children of English soldiers. But only two words haunted Sarah's thoughts, "kutcha butcha". She had impressed upon the boys, from an early age, that if she wasn't around and a stranger asked either of them where their mother was from, they must say, "She is from England".

Despite the distance, there was a fair amount of human traffic between Peshawar and Cherat. A near constant back and forth with supplies and equipment, and periodic movements of personnel. The regiment's senior officers were well aware that Peshawar was a far from ideal posting, particularly for men who had just spent three years at what amounted to a mountain resort. So to avoid any resentment and bad feeling developing amongst them, which would inevitably be directed towards NCOs, officers and the men working at Cherat, the commanders came up with a plan. They decided to send no more than 250-300 men from Peshawar to Cherat at a time, recalling these after six months, and replacing them with the same number. This seemed an ideal solution, as it addressed the issue of men being separated from their families for overly long periods and rewarded everyone for their work at Chakrata.

John arrived back at Peshawar at the end of August, having completed his first six-month stint in Cherat. He downplayed the place to Sarah and the boys, not wanting to make their own situation seem even worse by comparison. It was in early October that the first few people started falling ill at Chakrata. This barely registered in the camp at first. Diarrhoea and vomiting were hardly uncommon in India, and not something their victims felt inclined to talk about. When more people became ill and word got around, everyone assumed it was Peshawar Fever. However, within a couple of days of the first cases of sickness, people started dying. Some people would die within hours of becoming ill, others would be sick for a few days before succumbing. This wasn't Peshawar Fever, it was cholera. Carried back from Cherat, and spreading like wildfire in Peshawar due in large part to the insanitary conditions there.

Sarah was alone when she first began to feel ill on the afternoon of October 17, 1872. She was alone, John having taken the boys out for a walk around the camp. After feeling nauseous for a little while, she vomited. The vomit appeared to be slightly blood-flecked, but the redness could just as easily have come from something she had eaten. Then she was struck by a heavy bout of diarrhoea. This too appeared blood-flecked. Heavily so. Within an hour of first feeling unwell, Sarah was running a high temperature, constantly vomiting and diarrheic. Excruciating pains that had started in her stomach were now spreading across the rest of her body. When John arrived back with the children, he saw immediately that she was very ill, and turned to go back out the door. "I'll get a medic," he told her. But Sarah's main concern was for William and Jack. "No, we can't risk the boys becoming ill. Take them to stay with someone else," she whispered. Though he had no idea where to take them, John agreed and turned to William and Jack, "Come on boys, let's go for another walk."

They were walking through the camp when someone called out to John. He turned and saw Henry Pope coming towards them. Henry knew immediately by the look on John's face that something was wrong. As the boys played out of earshot, John explained the situation. "I'll take them. You go back to Sarah. She needs you," said Henry. As Henry walked away, hand-in-hand with the boys, John headed back to their mother. Along the way he began to feel nauseous. Then he vomited. He could hardly stand by the time he made it back to Sarah. "The boys are fine," he whispered, "They're with Henry." Then he climbed into bed beside her. Sarah smiled before losing consciousness. She clung to life for two days, before the cholera claimed her.

Sarah Adams died, aged 43, in Peshawar camp in the early hours of October 19, 1872. According to a doctor who was nearby, the last words she ever spoke were, "My boys. Please look after my boys."

John did not hear her. He did not get to say goodbye to the mother of his children, the love of his life. He was unconscious at the time, his body locked in its own battle with cholera. The last memory William and Jack were to have of their mother was her smiling over at them and saying, "Go walk with Papa, my loves. And have some fun." On the same day she died, Sarah was buried at Peshawar camp "by the officer on duty". *(11)* She was one of 20 women and children who would succumb to cholera over the next few weeks. Each buried in the camp within hours of dying.

Where are the boys?
The 55th, which only a few years earlier had been lauded by newspapers across the empire as a shining example of the British army at its best, was devastated by the cholera outbreaks at Peshawar and Cherat. A report in *The Englishman's Overland Mail* on January 03, 1873 described the "general appearance" of the men of the 55th as, "one of suffering", with between "20 to 30 per cent being either in hospital or just convalescent". Another publication, *The Broad Arrow*, was not quite as reserved in its use of language as the *Overland Mail*, and began referring to Cherat simply as "the cholera camp". How times had changed. A report from Chakrata in 1871 had remarked on the "obvious good health" of the men of the 55th.

John Adams was one of those who survived the cholera outbreak, and at the time of the *Overland Mail*'s report was slowly recovering in the camp's hospital. He had swung between unconsciousness and delirium for three weeks. Then the fever began to lift.

When John first began to recover, he had no idea where he was, or what had happened to him. After a short while he realised that he was in a hospital, and obviously very sick. "Where's my wife and children," he asked an orderly who was fussing about at his bedside, "Are they okay?" "You're very weak, so try not to talk," replied the orderly, "You need all the rest you can get." Then he disappeared. The orderly reported to the head doctor, a Captain Semple, what John had asked him, "What should I tell him, sir?" "Nothing," said Semple, "I'll deal with it."

Semple was not a man given to beating about the bush, and he certainly did not believe in trying to sugarcoat a bitter pill. That is not to say he was without empathy. Far from it. He just thought that one of the worst things a doctor can do is to raise false hope and expectations. "How are you feeling today, son," he asked John. This was the first time anyone had called him "son" since that day, now long ago, when he had joined the army at Newry. It unnerved him a little. "I'm fine, sir," he replied. "No, you're far from fine," said Semple, "You've just started on the road to recovery from a bout of cholera that nearly killed you. It's in that context I was asking how you are." "I need to know where my wife and children are, sir," said John. "I'm sorry, Adams, but I'm afraid your wife didn't make it. I don't know anything about your children, but I'll do my darnedest to find out for you. I really am sorry, son," and with that, Semple turned to walk away. John managed to contain himself long enough to blurt out, "Sergeant Pope will know, sir," before succumbing to agonies of sorrow and fear.

After they had left John, Henry took William and Jack by the hand, "Let's go for a walk, boys." The children sensed something wasn't right, "Why is papa not coming with us?" asked Jack. "He has to go to work," replied Henry. William said nothing. Wandering aimlessly through the camp, they would come upon little knots of people talking anxiously amongst themselves, while others would be scurrying back and forth with worried looks on their faces. "Can we go back to Mama now?" Jack asked. "Not yet for a while," said Henry, who had been dreading the question. What on earth am I going to do with them, he wondered. William walked along, looking around, still saying nothing. This went on for another hour or so. Henry tried to act natural with the boys, to excite their interest. All the while Jack was becoming more agitated, wanting to go back to his mother and father, and William remained silent.

A soldier came hurrying up to Henry, "Sarge, can I have a word." Henry took a few steps away from the boys, "Yes, what is it, corporal?" They spoke for a moment or two in hushed tones. Henry's dilemma had just got an awful lot worse. When he went back to the boys, Jack again started demanding to be taken back home. "Shut up, Jack," said William, and Jack immediately fell silent. William then turned to Henry, "Mama is sick isn't she, Henry." "Yes William, I'm afraid she is, son. And your father too," replied Henry, "You and Jack are going to have to stay with me for a little while." "Are they going to be all right?" asked William. "Yes, of course. I'm sure they'll be fine," replied Henry, far from convincingly. Jack said nothing. He just took William's hand, and held on tight to it.

John's recovery was slow and tortuous. The latter part not entirely due to the enormous physical stress his body had endured, and must now claw its way back from. The stronger he got the more the enormity of losing Sarah and not knowing what had happened to the boys weighed down upon him. Semple was as good as his word and, after making some enquiries, reported back to John, "I was unable to talk to Sergeant Pope directly, as I have been informed he travelled to Karachi and it will be some time before he is back. Pope is a good man, Adams. You couldn't have entrusted your children to a more capable person. So I wouldn't worry unduly about them, if I were you." Semple suspected more than he was telling John, but this was as far as he was prepared to go without being certain. He wasn't going to speculate.

One minute John would be full of hope, "Henry wouldn't let anything happen to the boys. He'll make sure they're all right". And the next he would be in a state of despair, "Sarah and I both caught the cholera, so how could the boys not have caught it too? Henry wouldn't be able to save them from that". He suspected Semple wasn't being totally honest with him. That the doctor knew more, but was waiting for John to regain some of his strength before bringing more terrible news.

John half-expected that one day he would look up to see Henry Pope walking through the door - come to tell him that William and Jack hadn't made it. Sometimes his darkest imaginings would become too much for him, and he would lie in his bed sobbing and crying openly. This was not the time for trying to maintain a soldierly, manly, take-it-on-the-chin demeanour.

After telling the boys that their parents were ill, Henry didn't think there was any point to maintaining the fiction of being out for a relaxing stroll, so he took William and Jack back to the sergeants' quarters. (One of the perks of being a sergeant was that you had a room to yourself.) He got the boys some food, which they only picked at, and then showed them where the latrine and wash basins were. "You're going to have to bed down here tonight, lads. 'Til we see in the morning how your mum and dad are doing," he told them. William and Jack nodded. "I'll be sleeping in a mate's room. It's just up the hallway. I'll show you where in a minute. If you need me in the middle of the night, come and knock on the door." Then he looked directly at William, "If either of you start feeling sick during the night, you have to come and tell me. Now that's very important. If you feel sick at all. Come and get me." The boys nodded again. After he had tucked them up in bed, and was headed for the door, Jack called out to him, "Are Momma and Papa going to be all right, Henry?" "I hope so, son. I really hope so," Henry replied. And with that he left them. Jack fell asleep clinging to William, and lay like that throughout the night.

The next day, after he was assured that neither of them was feeling ill, Henry gave the boys some breakfast and then left them in his room while he went on "an errand". He went first to check up on Sarah and John, and was told that it looked unlikely either would survive. It was one of the few times in his life that he felt scared. Very scared. After some thought, Henry went to ask the wife of a fellow sergeant if she would look after the boys for the day, while he figured out what to do.

The woman took a bit of persuading, given the cholera situation. But after being assured that they were showing absolutely no signs of sickness, she took pity on the boys (and on Henry) and agreed, "But I'll keep them for just this one day".

Henry had bought a little time, but that was all. And he was only too aware of the fact. What on earth was he going to do now? What if Sarah and John didn't make it? What would happen to the boys then? They were of mixed race, of an unsanctioned marriage. The army certainly wouldn't look after them. And even if there was the slimmest chance of finding local people that would take them in, which there wasn't, how would they ever survive? That was if they survived long enough for those issues to even arise. There was still the possibility, and a strong one, that they could go down with cholera themselves. His immediate worry, however, was what to do with them the following day.

Fortunately, when Henry went to collect the boys later that day it was clear his colleague's wife had taken a shine to them. He didn't even have to ask her to look after them again, she suggested it, "Such lovely youngsters. So well behaved. Bring them along tomorrow, if you need to." That night, after Henry had left the room and they were alone in bed, Jack began to cry, asking for his mother and father. William hugged him, "Don't worry, Jack. I'll look after you. We'll look after each other." Henry learned in the mid-morning of the next day that Sarah had died and been buried almost immediately after. He didn't say anything to the boys. He dropped them off at the friend's home, as planned, then went to enquire again after John. There was no change, he was still barely clinging to life. Henry really didn't know which way to turn. Then fate intervened.

A few weeks later, as John lay recovering from the effects of the cholera, and reflecting on Sarah and the boys, something struck him for the first time. Even if the boys had survived - which was beginning to feel more and more like a forlorn hope - and he was able to regain his full strength, how on earth was he going to look after them? He was a soldier and widower, the father of two mixed-race children, and stationed far distant from home. His marriage had never been recognised by the army, and, by extension therefore, neither had the existence of his children. So he could expect no help from that quarter. (Even if compassionate leave had existed at the time, and extended far enough down the military pecking order to someone as low-ranked as John, he would still not have been eligible. All because of officialdom's non-recognition of his marriage to Sarah.) What was he to do? What should he hope for? He tried pushing everything to the back of his mind in the hope that a solution would eventually come to him. But the problem of the boys refused to retreat into the background. It tortured him throughout his waking hours and haunted him as he slept.

One day, as he sat in a chair by his bed, head bowed in thought, he heard the opening of a door and looked up to see Sergeant Henry Pope enter the room, and make his way towards John's bed. Henry had been dreading this visit.

He pulled up a chair beside John and reached out and took his hand, "I'm so sorry about Sarah, my old friend. She was a wonderful woman, and I know how happy the two of you were". John thanked him. Then, with what would have been indecent haste in any other circumstances, "What about William and Jack, Henry? Where are my boys?"

"I'm sorry, John but...", and that was as far as Henry got before John broke down in tears, "Don't tell me they're gone too. Please don't tell me I've lost my sons as well, Henry." "No, no, they're alive and well," Henry almost shouted. "Oh, thank God for that," John shouted back "And thank you, Henry. What would we have done without you." Then he added, as if as an afterthought, "Where are they?" "That's the thing, John," sighed Henry, "I'm so sorry, I thought I had no choice, but they're... they're on their way to England, as we speak." "What are you apologising for," cried John, "That's wonderful news. Truly wonderful news." Henry's relief at John's reaction nearly matched that of his friend's upon learning that the boys were alive and well. He relaxed, and began to explain what had happened.

On the morning following Sarah's death, after he had dropped the boys off at the kindly woman's house and learned of John's perilous condition in hospital, Henry made his way to the sergeants' office, where an urgent message awaited him. He had to report immediately to the commanding officer, Major Duncan. He left immediately to find out what he had done wrong. Good God, this is all I need, he thought. Upon his arrival at the CO's office Henry was shuttled straight through to the inner sanctum, where he was greeted by the man himself, "Ah, Sergeant Pope, how are you my good man." Well, it looks like I'm not in trouble anyway, thought Henry, "I'm fine, thank you sir. And yourself?" Duncan didn't bother telling Henry how he was, but launched straight into the reason he had sent for him, "It's this damned cholera, Pope. We have to get the men out of here, a replacement battalion is already being organised." [A Sikh battalion would be the replacement. Considered expendable, presumably. Or at least, *more* expendable. *(12)*] Hardly pausing for breath, the CO continued, "But we need to get the women and children out of here first. They're dropping like damned flies. "I want you to take charge of everything. Grab as many fit men as you need, and get it done as soon as possible. Organise transport to Karachi for them all. If any of our own [by which he meant British] want to travel on home to England, then sort that out for them too. The rest will stay at our barracks in Karachi until further notice." He stopped talking for a moment to judge Henry's reaction, before enquiring, "Can you handle that for me, Sergeant?" "Yes, sir. I'll get on to it right away, sir," replied Henry, with the germ of an idea already forming in his head. "Thank you, Sergeant. I knew you were the right man for the job. Now don't let me hold you back," said Duncan by way of dismissing him. As Henry headed for the door, Duncan remembered something else and called out to him, "Oh and Sergeant, while you're about it. Any fit man with less than 18 months to serve, who has indicated that he won't be signing on again, send him home to England with the women and children. Might as well kill two birds, and all that." "Will do, sir," Henry responded, his idea taking shape all the time.

It didn't take long for Henry to get things moving. He picked four men to help him: a sergeant, a corporal and two privates. He set three of these to alerting all healthy women in camp that they and their children would be moving out within the next few days and were to be ready to leave at a couple of hours notice. The sergeant was tasked with making the logistical arrangements: finding out train times and arranging transport to and from the stations. Then, when he had the numbers of women and children that would be travelling, he would alert the rail people to ensure that however many carriages they needed would be set aside for them. Henry took it upon himself to list the names of the women and children, and the details of who amongst them would be travelling on to England. He did the same regarding the details of any soldiers who would be going to England with them. When all the listing, detailing, interviewing, and arranging had been completed, there were 208 healthy women and children to be evacuated. Of these, 15 women, 37 children, and three soldiers would be travelling on to England. Henry planned for there to be two more children going to England. But he was leaving it until Karachi, where neither he nor the evacuees were known personally, before moving two extra names across from the list of 208 where they presently sat, unnoticed.

One evening Henry sat William and Jack down to tell them about the death of their mother. "I'm so sorry, boys," he began. He got no further before William asked, "Has our mama died?" "Yes son, I'm afraid she has," answered Henry. Jack said nothing, but the tears began to run down his face. Then he began howling and sobbing, and crying out for his mother. William began crying too, but made no sound other than to ask, "And is our papa dead, too?" "No, but he is very ill," said Henry. William took his younger brother in his arms. And he and Jack sat wrapped together on Henry's bed crying and hugging, each in turn calling out for his mother. "What will become of us if Papa dies too," Jack asked his older brother. "Don't worry," said William, "Henry will look after us." Henry left the room for a few minutes to compose himself. He didn't want the boys to see him crying.

Two nights after breaking the news of Sarah and John to the boys, Henry sat them down again, and proceeded to tell them of his plan. When he had done, he kept repeating, "Now, whatever you do, remember what I told you. That's really important. Never, ever, ever, forget what I told you." They nodded. He then asked them a few questions as a test, and they passed with flying colours. All went well on the day of the evacuation. Henry had commandeered another 10 men to shepherd the women and children and help with the baggage. Himself and five of them, plus his four original helpers, would travel with the party to Karachi. Where they would hand over responsibility for the women and children who were staying in India to the army based there. Himself and his four original helpers would stay in the city to arrange voyage to England for the remaining 15 women and, by then, 39 children.

Henry needed someone to act as chaperone to the boys on the voyage to England and, just as importantly, to deliver them safely to their final destination. Again he was fortunate. Of the three soldiers travelling with the party, one was a thief ("couldn't trust him as far as you could throw him," was John's character assessment of him) another wasn't very bright ("more brains in an ammo box") but the third was perfect for what Henry had in mind ("as honest as the day is long"). An old sweat who had known Henry for years, James "Cloughie" Fairclough, was not only honest but as smart and worldly-wise as they come. When Henry put the plan to him, Cloughie volunteered right away, "No problem, Sarge. They'll be safe as houses with me." Henry gave Cloughie a sealed letter to deliver at the boys' destination in England. He gave him some money, and then had to force him to take another £1:00 for himself, to cover expenses and a little more besides.

When the women and children were being separated at Karachi, Henry removed the names of William Adams and John Henry Adams from the list of those bound for the military camp. And added the names of William Pope and John Henry Pope to the list of those who would be travelling to England. Their father was named as Sergeant Alfred Pope of the 55th (Westmorland) Regiment of Foot. And their mother was listed as Mary Pope, who had died of cholera at Peshawar camp. They would be travelling to England in the care of Private James Fairclough of the 55th.

Henry saw Cloughie and the boys off at Karachi, as they boarded the ship that would take them to Bombay, where they would take another ship to England. Just as they were about to part, Henry hugged William and Jack and said, "Now remember what I told you." "We will, Henry," they said in unison. Then he turned to their chaperone, "Now Cloughie, any trouble and you blame me. Tell them I threatened you and made you do it. I'll own up to it right away." Cloughie laughed at him, "As if I would, Sarge. As if I would." And with that they were gone. The next day, as they were about to board their England-bound ship at Bombay, Cloughie handed over some documents to the official checking the paperwork of boarding passengers. Then he spoke to him in a low whisper, as if to shield the boys from further hurt, "The poor little mites. Their mother died of the cholera. A lovely woman she was too, from Devon. Their father, the sarge, can't look after them so he's sending them home to his old mum to take care of. Heartbroken the little mites are. And so is the sarge, truth be told." The official looked genuinely moved. He leaned down and tussled Jack's hair, "And what's your name, little fella?" "John Henry Pope, sir," answered Jack, as easily as if it were his real name. The official nodded to Cloughie, "Okay, on you go. And safe voyage lads." Henry checked that all three had made it safely on to the ship for England before he again altered his paperwork. He changed the surnames of the boys and their supposed father from Pope to Pape, then he went to deliver two folders to Major Duncan.

The major flipped open each folder and made a note of the total numbers on a pad in front of him, "Well done, Sergeant. A damn fine job you've done here. I knew I could leave it to you." Duncan smiled to himself, this was how his superiors would congratulate him. "Thank you, sir," said Henry, a split second before the major dismissed him.

As Major Duncan was putting the files in a cabinet, never to be looked at again, at least not by anybody who had the faintest knowledge of the people whose names were listed there, Henry was on his way to see John in the hospital.

"You've saved their lives, Henry. You've saved my sons' lives. How can I ever repay you?" "Ha, ha, no need for that, John. You'd have done the same for me." Henry Pope had indeed saved the lives of Jack (5), and William (7), who were on their way to a new life in England, a country they had never set foot in before, and where they had not a single relative.

1) From numerous newspaper reports in late August, 1869: The Homeward Mail (August 23); the Edinburgh Evening Courant (August 24); Weekly Dispatch (August 29) et al, www.search.findmypast.co.uk
2) Report in Broad Arrow on November 25, 1871, www.search.findmypast.co.uk
3) Report in The Englishman's Overland Mail on April 24, 1877, www.search.findmypast.co.uk
4) Report in the Dundee Courier on November 05, 1877, www.search.findmypast.co.uk
5) Report in Broad Arrow on July 01, 1871, www.search.findmypast.co.uk
6) From January through July 1871 reports were carried in the Delhi Gazette; Broad Arrow; The Times of India; The Times of London et al, www.search.findmypast.co.uk
7) From a report in the Army and Navy Gazette of June 15, 1872, www.search.findmypast.co.uk
8) Irish Times article by Fintan O'Toole on August 24, 2021, https://www.irishtimes.com/opinion/fintan-o-toole-the-west-had-all-the-clocks-but-the-taliban-had-all-the-time
9) The Looming Tower: Al-Qaeda's Road to 9/11, by Lawrence Wright, published by Penguin Books (2011)
10) Reminiscences of Missionary Work in Amritsar 1872-1873 and on the Afghan Frontier in Peshawar 1873-1890, by the Rev. Worthington Jukes (1925), http://anglicanhistory.org/india/jukes1925/
11) From the official record of Sarah's death and burial, htttps://www.fold3.com
12) Army and Navy Gazette, November 23, 1872, www.search.findmypast.co.uk

Peshawar city, circa the 1870s

Extracts from John Adams' British Army attestation papers and his pension records

Records of Bella's baptism and burial

William's and Jack's baptismal records

Top: Record of Sarah's death and burial in 1872
Bottom: The British census returns of April 03, 1881 showed William and Jack (bottom entry) living at Long Sutton, Somerset under the surname of Pope

The British Army cantonment at Peshawar where, on October 19, 1872, Sarah died of cholera and, "Was buried in camp by the officer on duty".

Chapter 7

England
Cloughie and the boys got along famously. Like Henry, he had a way with children and found it easy to talk to them on their level. As soon as they boarded the ship at Bombay, he said to them, "Okay then, we have to be clear about something before we start. If this here boat sinks on the way to England, we're using William to keep us afloat in the sea. You just lie there in the water William, and me and Jack will cling on to you. No sense in the three of us being lost." Then he grinned, "What you say, Jack?" Jack laughed, "No Cloughie, me and William will cling on to you," and he took William's hand. When they got to their cabin, not much bigger than a large wardrobe, but better than what they expected, Cloughie sat the boys down and spoke seriously to them, "Now I know you're smart lads, but just in case one of you is

caught unawares and slips up. Don't make it too obvious, but try to steer clear of the women as much as possible. Some of them might know you or Sergeant Pope, and we don't want them asking awkward questions, now do we. Such as 'I thought you were called Adams'. Or maybe one of them'll say 'Sergeant Pope ain't married, so how come you two are his sons'. If one of them does collar you, just stick to the story. Your mother died. She was called Mary. And your father is Sergeant *Alfred* Pope. Be sure to say *Alfred* Pope that's part of his proper name, but they'll not know that. They'll think it's another Sergeant Pope you're talking about. If they ask, but only if they ask, your mother was English. You father is sending you home to your old grandma to take care of you. You don't know her. Never met her before." He looked at each of them in turn, "Okay boys, have we got that." "Yes, Cloughie," they responded in unison. He reached across and tousled each one's hair, "Good lads. Now let's see if we can find something to eat on this boat. I'm famished."

They needn't have worried about the women passengers. Any time they bumped into one she would do little more than smile and nod. Occassionally one would ask how they were keeping, but that was all. Doubtless the women had more than enough to occupy their minds, such as how they were going to resettle themselves and their children in England, without being concerned about other people's business.

The cabin may have been very small, but it had everything they needed. A latrine, a washbasin, and four bunks. The bunks were fixed in an L shape, with an upper and a lower one on each leg of the L. William took the upper bunk that lay just below a porthole, because he liked to look out at the sea. Jack took the one directly below him, for the opposite reason. Cloughie claimed the upper bunk of the remaining two. The three of them spent a lot of time in the cabin. Partly because they wanted to avoid the evacuee women, but also because the boys, particularly Jack, had become very quiet and seemingly uninterested in anything around them. Cloughie would insist at times that they all go up on deck to stand at the railings and watch out for whales, porpoises and whatever else they might see.

William and Jack would never raise any protest, but it was clear they were only going through the motions. It was the same with the stories of army life (heavily edited for a young audience) that Cloughie regaled them with. William would smile at all the right places, but his heart wasn't in it. Jack just sat looking bored. They were missing their mother terribly; missing and worrying about their father; and dreading going to live in England. A place they had barely heard about before, much less spent any time in. They were also wrestling with the knowledge that they were somehow considered lesser beings than other army children. Jack would say to William, "I don't want to go to England. I just want to go home." Sometimes he would suddenly burst into tears, and cry out for his mother. William began sharing the bottom bunk with his little brother, hugging him until he slept.

As the ship crawled along on its journey, edging ever closer to the depths of a British winter, the days gradually got shorter and colder, and the nights longer and colder still. By the time England (just about) appeared on the horizon, slightly less than a month after they had left Bombay, icy rain was pouring down and a freezing wind was blowing what felt like a gale. The trio joined the other passengers lined up along the railings to catch a sight of their destination. This, for the vast bulk of them, was their homeland.

There were intermittent cheers each time snapshots of the land appeared out of the rain, but they were rather half-hearted. Perhaps the other people were feeling the same as Cloughie was. After close to 20 years overseas, most of his time spent in India, he was shivering with the cold, thinking that he hadn't seen a more depressing sight in a very long time. But that was nothing to how William and Jack were feeling. They loved when the rains came in India, so soft, warm and refreshing. But this rain was different; bitterly cold, it attacked you and froze you to the core. And everything was so dark and gloomy. "I want to go home," Jack mouthed to his brother. "So do I," said William.

The ship docked at Southampton, and in less than two hours Cloughie and the boys were standing on a platform at Southampton Terminus rail station, waiting for a train to Taunton in Devon. The officials checking the new arrivals off the ship had barely glanced at each set of documents thrust in front of them. Presumably trusting that their counterparts in Bombay had been meticulous.

When they left the train at Taunton they caught a bus that took them just over the county border to a small village in Somerset, Long Sutton. With the passing of every mile, William and Jack slipped deeper and deeper into a depressed state. Everything was so foreign to them. From the places to the people. From the weather to the smells. Compared to the almost constant sunshiny brightness of India, its profusion of colours, its odours of herbs and spices, England seemed so rundown and decrepit. What will become of us, William wondered to himself. Jack was long past wondering anything. He had entered a semi-comatose state, just gazing with speechless terror at all before him. Everywhere the boys looked there were white people. Hordes of them. But totally unlike the white people they were used to. The English variety was almost invariably chalk-white and ill-looking.

Long Sutton

Long Sutton was a tiny village, so Cloughie soon found the house he was looking for and knocked on the door. It was opened by an elderly but sprightly looking woman, not much shorter than Cloughie (who stood 5ft - 6ins tall), with one of those faces that perfectly reflects the character of the person behind it. She looked like a kindly, decent sort, and was indeed both of those things, and a bit more besides. She was also shrewdly intelligent and expert at reading other people.

As she swung open her door, Mrs Pope appeared on the verge of tears, "Oh my goodness, what has happened to my Henry," she immediately asked, "Is he all right? Please tell me he's all right." She had watched from the window of her front room as a soldier stopped outside, took an envelope from his pocket, and approached the door. She assumed the two boys with him were locals who had been directing him to where she lived. "Now, now, Mrs Pope, no need for you to worry and upset yourself, the sarge is fine," said Cloughie, at the same time thinking, this isn't a bad turn of events, what I've got to tell her will seem like good news in comparison to what she feared.

Cloughie handed her £2:00 and the sealed letter, "These are from the Sarge. He has explained everything here." She took it, while telling him, "I can't even read." "Then I'll explain it all to you. "You can have someone trustworthy read the letter to you at another time," said Cloughie. "Oh what am I thinking. Come in, come in," she ordered the three of them. Mrs Pope ushered Cloughie and the two boys over the door and into the front room from where she had been watching their approach. There was a fire blazing in the grate. She sat them down, Cloughie in an armchair and the boys on the floor, telling them to sit closer to the fire to warm themselves. She then sat herself down in a large armchair, and Cloughie began telling her the full story of how they came to be there. Every so often she would interject with comments like "Oh, the poor woman" or, looking over at the boys, "Oh, isn't that terrible". Before Cloughie had finished, she motioned the boys over, threw her arms around them and pulled them close, "Oh you poor boys. Don't worry, I'll look after you now." They snuggled in to Mrs Pope. It was the first in a long time that William and Jack had felt safe. When Cloughie had finished, she gave them bread and cold beef for supper. Afterwards she explained the arrangements for the night, "William and Jack, you two will sleep on the couch tonight, and I'll get some sort of beds fixed up for you tomorrow. Mr Fairclough, you'll have to make do with the floor, I'm afraid. I'll get you all some blankets. And there's plenty of coal there Mr Fairclough, so keep the fire burning all night or you'll catch your deaths in this cold."

The next morning, after breakfast, Cloughie took his leave of them, and headed for his hometown of Lancaster. He hugged each of the lads in turn and wished them luck, "You'll be fine here with Mrs Pope, she seems a good sort." "Thanks for looking after us, Cloughie," said William. "Bye, bye, Cloughie. And thank you," said Jack. Then, with a thank-you to Mrs Pope and a shake of her hand, Cloughie was gone.

John's recovery from cholera was slow. His body had been taken almost beyond its limits of endurance by the disease, and would take a long time to recover. He was constantly thirsty and had trouble keeping his food down, often vomiting or suffering from diarrhoea whenever he ate something. The slightest exertion would tire him out. After Henry's visit he spent another month in hospital before being discharged, fit only for "light duties". These amounted to him continuing his recuperation in the barracks (as he no longer had married quarters), engaging in duties only when he felt up to it, and only for as long as he wanted. He was physically exhausted, and it was a year before he began to feel anything like how he had been before being struck down by cholera. He was emotionally exhausted too, and never recovered fully from that. He missed Sarah and the boys terribly, and was tortured with guilt. "Was it me that brought the cholera back from Cherat that killed Sarah?" ; "Did I rob the boys of their mother?"; "What sort of father is it anyway, that has his youngsters living with strangers in a far-off country?"

John wasn't worried about the boys' everyday welfare, as such. They had to be in safe hands with Henry's mother. Only a decent person could raise a son to turn out like him. But he did worry about their happiness. They had lost their mother, and, in the process, their father, and were being forced to adjust to a life completely alien to them. Most of all, John was tormented by the fear that their mixed-race background would be discovered. What would become of William and Jack if that happened? When would he see them again? Would he *ever* get to see them again? Henry and other of his friends would try to cheer him up and, appreciating their efforts, he would play along with them a bit. But they could see he was a tortured soul.

It was well into 1874 before John regained full fitness, which was only a little under two years short of when his 21 years in the army would be up. He pushed in another year, doing the usual everyday things that he and thousands like him were accustomed to. Parades, drill, guard and sentry duties, rifle practice, and innumerable odd-jobs around the camp that required doing. He continued to be the good and reliable soldier he had always been, but his heart was no long in it. In April 1875, he was told that he would soon be sent to England to see out the last year or so of his service at the 55th's regimental headquarters in Carlisle. John was elated. Now he would finally get to see his boys again.

Mrs Pope had the letter from her son that Cloughie had delivered read to her by a younger sister of Henry's, Josephine. In it, Henry recounted the story of Sarah, John and the boys just as Cloughie had told it, and asked his mother if she would look after William and Jack until other arrangements could be made. Henry didn't hint at what "other arrangements" he might have in mind, for the very good reason that he hadn't thought of any. His main objective had been to get the boys out of India to somewhere safe. He hadn't considered anything beyond that. When the boys were gone, and Henry knew John would survive, it made perfect sense to let them remain in Somerset with his mother until their father could collect them when he left the army in four years. However, four years is a very long time in the life of child. Neither Henry nor John took any account of how well settled in Somerset William and Jack might become over that period.

From the moment Cloughie left her house, Mrs Pope treated the boys as though they were her own. She fitted out a small back upstairs bedroom for them: mattress on the floor, plenty of blankets, and a small chest of drawers for their belongings. From the money Henry had sent, she bought them clothes more suited to the English weather than those they had brought with them: jackets, shirts, wooly socks and jumpers, and sturdy shoes. As soon as the Christmas holidays were over, the first Christmas in any real sense that the boys had ever celebrated, Mrs Pope enrolled William at the local school, as her grandson. She was well-liked and highly-respected in the village, so this presented no problem. She worked as a housekeeper for a local magistrate, so it was arranged that Josephine would look after Jack during the day, until he was old enough to be enrolled at school.

Mrs Pope was kind but firm with the boys. She would shower them with praise and attention, and lots of food. She loved to bake, and was very accomplished at it. What had been born of necessity when her children were young was something she now took great joy from, and pride in. The house was seldom without the smell of baking bread, buns, tarts or cakes. And William and Jack became the chief beneficiaries. She treated them as a mother, but never tried to supplant their actual mother. Indeed she took pains not to. She insisted they call her Nanna, and would refer to herself as "your old grandmother".

Mrs Pope had not, in fact, been anything like as relaxed about the prospect of caring for William and Jack as it appeared to Cloughie. A widow, getting on in years, set in her ways and used to living alone, her own children long ago grown and left home, she wasn't sure that she was still capable of rearing children. Moreover, capable or not, she wasn't sure that she wanted to take on the responsibility; or was prepared to have her life disrupted in the way that it surely would be by the sudden injection of two children into it. The thought of turning William and Jack away never entered her mind, of course. But she clung to the idea that it was a temporary arrangement. Henry had said as much in his letter when he wrote "until other arrangements can be made". So at the beginning she set about making the boys as comfortable as she could, providing for their needs, and getting to know them. All the while looking forward to an Irish relative of their's arriving at her door to take them off her hands. Gradually, as the weeks went past, and she got to know William and Jack, Mrs Pope realised that she actually enjoyed looking after them. She felt invigorated. Her life had new purpose. More than anything else, though, she came to love the boys as if they were her own. Far from looking forward to an Irish relative appearing, she began to dread it. Then, as the weeks of waiting became months, she began to relax and the dread in her subsided. It had become clear that there were no "other arrangements" and the boys would be staying with her.

William and Jack would sometimes chat to one another in Urdu, but only when they thought there was no one else around. They were chatting one day while alone in the sitting room when Mrs Pope arrived at the door and overheard them. She stood still for a few moments listening before they noticed her. "My, my, but that's a beautiful language," she said, "What is it?" "It's from home, Nanna," said Jack. William supplied a little more detail, "It's our Mama's. It's how we used to talk with her." Mrs Pope smiled, sat down on the couch, and motioned for the boys to sit on either side of her. She put an arm around each of them, "That is so nice, my darlings. You will always have the language that she taught you to remember your dear mother by. You must never, ever forget it." And they never did. Nor did they ever forget, or allow themselves to forget, their true status, or lack of it, in England. In modern parlance, they were illegal aliens. They agreed on a secret codeword, "Kutcha", if they ever felt in danger of being exposed, or if one believed the other might be relaxing his guard too much.

At a time when smacking was considered almost as essential to a child's upbringing as food and water, Mrs Pope was quite unique in that she had never raised her hand to a child in her life. She had other methods of instilling discipline and good behaviour. William and Jack soon learned that a request delivered in a soft voice and with a good-natured smile was in fact an order. An order that she expected to be carried out. She might say, "William, would you like to fetch some coal for the fire, please. That's a good boy," or "Jack, would you like to put your toys away now, and get ready for bed". A single complaint would be tolerated, as long as the request was then carried out. But a refusal to do as she asked would result in someone being sent to their room for an hour or two, or toys being confiscated for a few days. As a naturally even-tempered, biddable child, William adapted almost immediately. Though Jack, not quite so readily. For the older child, confrontation had always been a last resort. For the younger, it was never far removed from being his first. But Jack was nothing if not a quick learner. After a few toys had been confiscated and a few evenings were spent sitting alone in his bedroom, he soon learned to do as he was asked. Besides, Jack didn't like to displease Nanna, for he and William soon came to love her as much as she loved them. Jack liked the order and predictability of life with Nanna. He liked going to bed at night feeling safe and secure, and getting up in the morning knowing what the day would bring. What he learned from Nanna would stand him in good stead throughout his life. He never entirely lost his combative nature, or too far beyond the notion that he was always right and others must bend to his will. But he learned there were only a few things worth taking a stand over, and that most others weren't. He never would allow himself to be bullied, no matter the cost or how intimidating the bully. But this is hardly an uncommon trait amongst men of small stature, whose number the adult Jack would join.

As naturally amiable, biddable and diplomatic as he was, and would remain so all of his life, William too would never allow himself to be bullied. When he really believed in something he would dig his heels in and not budge an inch. He always saw the best in people, but he was never blind to the worst in them either. In short, he was nobody's fool. Nanna's daughter, Josephine, who was married and had two children of her own, was physically unlike her mother, being a few inches shorter and of a somewhat heavier build. She was not quite as tolerant of dissent in children as her mother. But aside from that they were essentially the same character.

Josephine, whose husband worked as farm labourer, lived just up the street, and would take Jack there when she was looking after him. He grew to love Josephine (or Aunt Josie, as he called her) almost as much as he did Nanna.

Being so much younger, Aunt Josie was, naturally enough, a fitter and more active version of Nanna. She and her two girls, both younger than five-year-old Jack, would often play hide 'n' seek, ring-a-ring-a-roses, or hide-the-parcel with him. In the summer months, when they could go outdoors, it would be hop-scotch, rounders or tag. Though it was far from their intended purpose, Jack learned a little more about the beauty of compromise and seeing another person's point of view through playing these games with Aunt Josie and the girls. He learned from four-year-old Rosie in particular, who took no nonsense, especially when it came to her younger sister, "No, Jack. It's not your turn. Eliza hasn't had her turn yet." Jack was not a bad child. Far from it. Nor had he been in any way badly raised before Somerset. Sarah was well aware that he needed more disciplining than William, and had begun the process. But suddenly she was gone. Considering everything he had been through, the wonder is that Jack was not damaged beyond repair by the time he landed in England.

The primary school was not far from Nanna's house, just a few hundred yards, but it might as well have been on another planet where the treatment of children was concerned. Master Parsons, the headteacher, couldn't have been more unlike Mrs Pope and Josephine if he had tried. Parsons ruled his little domain with a rod of iron (or a rod of cane, to be precise). He appeared to believe that a day should not be allowed pass without the thrashing of at least one child. Parsons' attitude to teaching, and children in general, was not so much "spare the rod and spoil the child" as "spare the rod and destroy the child". At least two or three children were thrashed at his school every day.

His subordinates, Miss Copeland and Mrs Wells, were almost as afraid of him as the pupils. Though they too could resort to violence, albeit not as often or to the same degree as their superior. Still, a child that displeased them might be cuffed around the back of the head with an open hand or a book, or have his or her knuckles rapped with a ruler. The worst offenders, according to their interpretation of what constituted an offence, they sent to Parsons for him to deal with.

The children that Parsons, Copeland and Wells had the least time for were those not academically gifted (though that isn't the terminology any of them would have used to describe them). When countless beatings about various parts of the body and numerous thrashings of the cane had failed to improve the ability of such children, they were simply ignored. They would sit all day in a classroom, looking around them and gazing out the window, and, provided they didn't make a noise or in any other way disrupt the class, the teacher would totally ignore them. At times they would be sent outside to sweep the yard, cut grass, gather leaves, or undertake some other mundane task. A child sent to work outside would at first rush to complete his or her job, hoping to please the teacher. But they soon learned to take their time. What pleased teacher most was not having them close by. The other children envied these virtual pariahs. But only until later in life. It was into this world that William, aged seven years and five months, was thrust in January 1873. His teacher, Miss Copeland, was a tall thin middle-aged spinster. Thankfully for him, William was not only an obedient child, but also bright and a quick learner. And he had received some schooling in India, so the experience was not entirely new to him (even if the methods were). Something else was in his favour, Miss Copeland knew Mrs Pope from church circles. Well enough to know not to cross her. And that she wouldn't be one to remain silent if she suspected her grandson was being mistreated.

William was a bit of a novelty to the other children at first. "You're from India?" asked a wide-eyed little girl, "is that in Devon?" Her geographical limitations were matched by William's, who responded, cautious as ever, "No, I'm not *from* there, it's where I was born. Where's Devon?" But all the children were impressed with the new boy. Some were jealous of the attention he was getting. And one boy in particular, Arnold Hargreaves, wasn't going to put up with it. He decided to bring this new arrival down a peg or two. Arnold began by sneaking up behind William, and pinching him. When the only reaction this provoked was a shrug and a smile from his target, Arnold decided that more was needed. He started bumping into William then pushing him a few times, claiming that William had bumped into him. One day as they were leaving school, Arnold did it again. But this time William stepped to one side and punched him square in the face. They began to fight, each giving as good as he got. The other children gathered round, cheering and shouting excitedly, as the two boys rolled about on the ground punching and tearing at one another. Hearing the commotion, Master Parsons ran over and dragged them apart. He held the two of them up by the scruffs of their jackets, "Rolling around in the street like two dogs. Fighting like animals, the pair of you. I'll soon put a stop to that." And he marched them off, still by the scruffs of their necks, to his office. Once there, he made each boy bend over, and caned him six times across the backside. When he had done, he dismissed them like... well, the dogs he considered them to be only marginally better than. Afterwards, Arnold and William walked homewards together, their clothes muddy and dishevelled, backsides aching, and faces dirty and tear-stained. They were friends after that day, and no other boy was ever tempted again to try and bully William. When he explained to Nanna why he was in such a state, she was angry at Parsons, "that man shouldn't be allowed to beat children", and philosophical about Arnold, "no wonder the child is violent, with what he's witnessed in the home he comes from".

It would appear that Mrs Pope was ahead of her time. Ahead of it by more than two centuries on her first point, and the clock is still ticking on her second.

School work didn't pose any great problems for William. He was soon doing as well as could be expected for a child of his age; mastering the basics of reading, writing and arithmetic. In August 1874, Jack joined him. Nanna and Josie worried about Jack starting school. He was a far happier and more disciplined child than when he had arrived in Long Sutton nearly two years before. But he still needed sympathetic handling, and they knew there was precious little chance of that at Mr Parson's school.

But they needn't have worried about Jack. He was a model pupil from the outset. Both in his behaviour and, being every bit as bright as William, in his progress. Thanks to William, Jack had been well prepared. Every evening for the past year, William had been taking him through all that he had been taught that day. He had also made Jack fully aware of what the teachers were like, what was expected of the pupils, and the punishments for bad behaviour. Most remarkable of all, for the first time in her professional life, and for reasons known only to herself, Miss Copeland took a shine to one of her pupils. And that pupil happened to be Jack. She didn't exactly fawn over him, that would have been too much. But she did occassionally smile at him, and even ruffled his hair one time while leaning over to examine some work of his. And never once did she raise her voice to Jack, much less threaten or strike him. Jack sailed through his first year at school, and was halfway into his second when his father arrived in Long Sutton to take him and his brother "home".

In early July 1875, John arrived in England, having been sent back from India to serve out his last 10 months in the army at the 55th's regimental headquarters at Carlisle. *(1)* He was glad to leave India. It held too many painful memories. Once in England he was determined there would be no more looking back. It's time now, he thought, to keep looking forward. Another nine months and he would be able to collect his sons. John had not written to the boys since he last saw them. If challenged on this, he might have tried to claim that he didn't want to upset or unsettle them in their new home, where they would have to remain for some years. He might even have said that he didn't know the exact address of the house where they were staying (Henry Pope had long since left for Ceylon [now Sri Lanka]). But the truth was he just couldn't face sitting down to write the letter. He had pushed the tragedies of losing Sarah and his sons to the back of his mind, and wanted them to remain there until he could at least deal with the second. John had simply concentrated on daily tasks in the knowledge that every day he managed to push in edged him closer to when he would be re-united with his boys.

He was in Carlisle a full six months before he sought permission to travel to Somerset, despite being fully aware that it would have been granted at any time. He had kidded himself that he might not be able to find the boys - as though Long Sutton was a grand metropolis, rather than the tiny village of circa 300 people that Henry had described. Henry hadn't written home since the letter to his mother that Cloughie had delivered. He considered his role to be finished, and, if he thought about it at all, that John would contact the boys to let them know of his recovery.

William and Jack were unaware of any of this. They presumed John was dead, as did everyone else. They had loved their father and would think of him, of course. But only occassionally. And less so as time passed. This was in stark contrast to their mother, who they still missed terribly and would regularly speak to one another about. Much as they loved Nanna and Aunt Josie, neither could ever take the place of their mother (not that either woman ever tried to). The boys never referred to the women's houses, and certainly not to Long Sutton, as home. When they spoke of home, they meant India.

One morning in mid-January 1876, Josie heard someone knocking at a door on her street, and looked out to see a man standing outside her mother's house. She shouted to him, "There's no one at home. Can I help you?" "I'm looking for Mrs Pope," replied the man, in an Irish accent. Josie was by now standing in front of him, "I'm her daughter, maybe I can help." He reached out to shake her hand and said, "Hello, I'm John Adams. I've come to collect my sons." Josie almost fainted. She brought John to her house and listened to his story.

Being assured that he actually was who he said he was, she told him how well the boys were doing, and how happy they were, all things considered. "We thought you were dead. Thank the Lord that my mother wasn't home when you called. She would have died on the spot," she said, "She'll be home presently, best you sit here for a while until she does. Let me tell her first, then I'll come and get you. She'll most likely collapse when she hears you're alive and well. And then there's the boys. They'll be delighted, obviously. But it'll be a big shock for them too."

Then she asked the obvious question, "Why haven't you been in touch before this?" John began his "didn't want to upset them" excuse, but seeing Josie's slightly incredulous expression, he stopped halfway through, hung his head for a few seconds and admitted, "I just couldn't face it." She nodded and said, sympathetically, "I understand", even though she didn't entirely.

Once Mrs Pope had recovered from the shock of hearing about the new arrival, Josie fetched John to meet her. "I can't thank you enough for taking William and Henry in, Mrs Pope," John told her, "Only for you and Henry, and Josie here of course, I don't know what would have become of them. You've been so kind. Words fail me." Wiping tears from her eyes, Mrs Pope replied, "No need for thanks, Mr Adams. It's been a pleasure. An absolute pleasure. We'll be so sorry to see them go. We've come to love William and Jack like our own. They're such a credit to you and your poor late wife." The subjects of this discussion had yet to appear and express a view on the latest development in their lives. As it was arranged that John would once again wait in Josie's house while mother and daughter explained to William and Jack what had happened. "We'll have to break this very gently to the little pets," said Mrs Pope, "It'll be a big shock for them. A good shock. But a shock nonetheless." John agreed.

When the boys trooped into the house after school, Nanna was her usual self. She busied around them, offering cakes and insisting they change their jumpers and trousers so she could wash them for school again the next day. Meanwhile, Josie would interrupt with questions on how school had been that day.

When everyone was settled, Nanna suddenly raised the subject of the boys' father, "Do you ever think about your pappa? We never did hear for definite whether he survived the cholera or not." Jack looked at her, wondering what had given rise to this line of questioning, "We know he died, Nanna. Why do you ask?" "But we don't know for sure," said Josie, "Wouldn't it be just wonderful if he had survived." William looked at Nanna, then Josie, then Nanna again, "Have you heard something? Is Pappa alive?" Jack was canny enough to sense that Nanna and Josie would not raise false hopes only to dash them again, "He is alive, isn't he?" "Yes, he is," said Nanna, "Your father is alive." Both boys let out whoops of joy. "Are you sure, Nanna? Are you sure?" William shouted in a pleading voice at Nanna. "Yes, we're certain, William," said Josie, "In fact he's in my house at this very moment, waiting to see you both." Jack froze for a moment, "Does this mean that Mama might still be alive, too?" he asked. "No, my pets," said Nanna, "I'm afraid, not." "How can you be sure?" demanded Jack, "If Pappa is alive then Mama might be too." "We're certain, Jack," said Josie. Nanna and Josie looked at one another. This wasn't something they had expected. Nanna nodded at Josie, and the younger woman made for the door. "Well, what are we waiting for," said Nanna, "Josie's going to fetch your father now."

The boys rushed to greet their father as he came through the door. John crying and hardly able to speak, hugged his sons to his chest. He had dreamed of this moment for so long. William and Jack kept repeating, "Oh Pappa, oh Pappa, you're alive." John couldn't believe how the boys had grown. In his mind they had remained the four- and six-year-olds of when he last saw them. But here they were now, Jack nearly eight and William nearly ten. So tall. Speaking over one another in their excitement, they asked a hundred questions of him. He told them all about his recovery and explained why he hadn't been in touch, "I knew it would be years before we saw each other again, and I didn't want to upset you while you were settling in with Mrs Pope and Josie." When he said this out loud he realised how ludicrous it sounded. But apparently not to the boys, who nodded in agreement. "It's Nanna and Aunt Josie," Jack corrected him. "Is Mama really dead then, Pappa," asked William. "Yes son, Mama is really dead. But she's looking down on us from somewhere, and she'll be really happy that we're back together again. And that I've come to take you home with me." "Home, home, we're really going home?" exclaimed Jack, "Oh, I'm so happy." "Yes son, we're really going home," John confirmed to him. William couldn't speak, but just stood with an enormous grin on his face. Nanna brushed away a tear, she was delighted for the boys but sad at the prospect of losing them. "When can we go home?" William asked his father. "Well, I have only a few more months until I'm finished in the army. Then I'll come and collect the two of you and we'll all travel up to Liverpool and get a boat from there to Ireland." The boys were stunned. They went silent for what seemed like an age, then Jack spoke, "Ireland? Why Ireland? You said we were going home." Josie and Nanna looked at one another, then the mother spoke, "Me and Josie will leave you three alone for a while. Let you catch up and make your plans." She tousled William's hair on her way past him to the door. Josie did the same with Jack. When the women had left, John, not yet grasping the seriousness of the situation, lightly explained, "Ireland is our home. That's where we're from, and we'll be going back to live there." "India is our home," declared Jack, his face like stone, "That's where we're from. Not Ireland." William nodded, "Yes

Pappa, India is our home. If we can't go back to India we want to stay here with Nanna and Aunt Josie."

After half-an-hour of trying without success to sell Ireland to the boys, John sought the help of the two women. After another hour of arguments and coaxing, the boys still wouldn't budge. If they couldn't go home to India, they wanted to stay where they were, with Nanna and Aunt Josie. Then John made his first big mistake, "Nanna and Josie have been more than good to you and me already, boys. They've looked after you for four years, for goodness sake. We couldn't possibly ask them to keep you on after I leave the army. Isn't that right, Nanna?" Nanna responded with a distinctly non-committal answer. It was obvious that she would love the boys to remain with her. William and Jack picked up on this right away, of course. After a bit more toing and froing, John and Nanna retired to the kitchen to have a word, while Josie stayed with the boys. "This has been a big day for them," Nanna said to John, "Maybe too big for them to take in. For years they thought you were dead, then you turn up out of the blue. They've always had their hearts set on returning to India and now they find they'll have to go to Ireland to live. Maybe best to leave it a few days, let it all settle into their little minds." John agreed, "Yes, I'll give it one more go, and if that doesn't work, I'll leave it a while. I've a few more months before I leave the army, anyway. Plenty of time." He was about to make his second, this time much greater, mistake.

It wasn't as if William and Jack had any great love for Long Sutton, but Nanna and Aunt Josie were there, both of whom they loved dearly. It wasn't that Long Sutton was a bad place to live, quite the opposite. It was a lovely village with more than its fair share of decent people, it just wasn't home to the boys. Neither did they have any strong attachment to particular friends at school. But at least they knew everyone at the school, pupils and teachers, and were settled there. They hated the weather in England, but Ireland's weather would be no better. In effect, their father was asking them to move to a place similar to where they already were. Except it didn't have Nanna and Aunt Josie, or anyone else that they knew. It would be like starting over again for them.

It's almost certain the boys wouldn't have agreed to go to live in Ireland, anyway. But by his own stupidity John made sure that they wouldn't. Following his chat with Nanna in the kitchen, he suddenly announced to the boys, as though delivering an unexpected Christmas gift, "And sure you'll get to meet your big sister in Ireland." There was a deathly silence. "We don't have a big sister," said William. "Yes you do, I was keeping her as a surprise for you," said John, a silly grin on his face. There followed another deathly silence.

Eliza Jane

John had of course told Sarah about the daughter he left behind in Ireland. But, understandably enough, he had never mentioned her to the boys. At their age, why would he? Time enough for that discussion after he had thought of a way to bring his family back to Ireland with him. But then fate intervened. The child's name, though no longer a child by 1876, was Eliza Jane. Her mother, also Eliza Jane, a daughter of James McClean, was from a family of weavers who lived in the Comber area of County Down. Being a weaver himself, John and Ms McClean had begun an on-off relationship after meeting at a weavers fair. Eliza Jane, born sometime in 1852, was the result. *(2)*

When Ms McClean fell pregnant, John had half-heartedly offered to "do the right thing" by her and the child. Half-heartedly, because she was 12 years older than him, 34 to his 22. As it happened, Ms McClean wasn't too enthusiastic about his offer, but was careful not to rebuff him immediately. A neighbour of hers, another weaver by the name of James Sturgeon, had also proposed to the expectant mother, promising to raise the unborn child as his own. Ms McClean wanted to be certain of Sturgeon's intentions before breaking with John. He did indeed prove to be sincere, and on August 03, 1853, Eliza Jane McClean and James Sturgeon were married at Moneyrea Presbyterian Meeting House. *(3)* John joined the army less than two years later, having barely formed a relationship with his daughter. But he never forgot her either. Eliza Jane was raised mainly by her mother's family, and while staying with them her surname was Adams. Over the years she would occassionally live with her mother and step-father, during which times she would adopt, or would be given, the surname of Sturgeon. Throughout her life, Eliza Jane would alternate between Adams and Sturgeon. A relatively minor deception, usually a means of avoiding embarrassment. There were a lot of McClean sisters, and she was particularly close to one of them, (Aunt) Martha, who was only 11 years older than herself.

With a degree of naïveté not uncommon in a grown man trying to deal with the emotions of children, John had thought the existence of a "big sister" in Ireland would convince William and Jack of familial roots there. Even make them eager to travel to meet her. Instead, he made them feel like they had been terribly deceived and betrayed by him. Seeing their reaction, or non-reaction more like, and despite never having met the adult Eliza Jane himself, John grasped for positives, "You'll love her when you meet her." Then excuses, "I never mentioned her before because you were so young." But it was a waste of time, and he knew it. In fairness, he could hardly go into a detailed explanation of the circumstances of Eliza Jane's existence to children so young. But even if he could have, it would have made no difference. No excuses or explanations would be accepted. It was the simple fact of her existence that hurt so much. "I don't want to meet her," was William's response. Jack was even more emphatic, "We don't want a sister." William was more adaptable to the vagaries of life than his younger brother, and much more forgiving. In time he would come to accept Eliza Jane, and move on. For Jack, however, a gulf had been created between him and his father that evening in Long Sutton. One that would never be entirely bridged.

After failing to convince the boys to come to Ireland with him, John was at a loss what to do next. He and Nanna had another discussion in the kitchen. "I don't know what to do, Mrs Pope. I can't force them to come to Ireland with me, and I can't just up and leave them here with you either." Nanna thought for a moment, and then spoke, "William and Jack have been through an awful lot, John. I don't have to tell you that. They're your sons, and if you want to take them to Ireland with you, then that's your right. But it wouldn't *be* right, if you get my meaning. They're settled here and doing well. Taking them to Ireland against their wishes would set them back goodness knows how much. And they might turn completely against you. Let them stay here for a while longer. Until they're a bit older. They'll love you for it, mark my words." John looked at her, "If you're sure you don't mind looking after them." Nanna laughed, " I love looking after them." John hugged her, "Thank you so much, Mrs Pope. No wonder Henry turned out to be such a fine man." John gave her some money towards the boys' upkeep, and arranged to come back again to see her and them before he left for Ireland.

When John announced to William and Jack that they would be staying in Long Sutton, after all, the atmosphere in the house changed immediately. It was as though a dark cloud had been lifted. The boys hugged and thanked their father, with Ireland and the "big sister" forgotten, at least for a while. They chatted to him about school, constantly sung the praises of Nanna and Aunt Josie, and told him of their journey from India with Cloughie. "Mama would be very proud of you. Her two boys," he said at one point, and meant it. Sarah would indeed be very proud.

John stayed the night at Nanna's, before heading back to Carlisle the next morning. As he was about to leave, he told the boys, "I'll be back to see you in a month or two, before I go home to Ireland." Jack gave him a questioning look. "Don't worry," laughed John, "I'll not be asking you to come with me." After he had left, things continued much as before at Long Sutton. William settled a little bit more, though he never let go of India. In a sense, Jack settled too. Though he couldn't have articulated it himself, he became more content with what he was doing - marking time.

Back To Annahilt

On May 17, 1876, 46-year-old John Adams left the British Army after 21 years, with his Crimea and service medals and four Good Conduct Badges. He had served 19 years and eight months of his time abroad (15 years and six months of it in India). As promised, he travelled down to Long Sutton to see William and Jack, and stayed with them for a week. It was like old times, except for the absence of Sarah, of course. But she was there in one sense at least. The boys talked more about Sarah to someone besides each other than they had done since she died. And it was the same with John. Each of them enjoyed being able to talk about her to others who had known and loved her as much as himself. After the week was up, it was time for tearful goodbyes. John made arrangements to send regular money to Mrs Pope, and he and the boys promised to write to one another. Then he left for Liverpool to catch a boat to Belfast.

John stated on his army attestation papers that he intended to live in Belfast after leaving the service. If that was indeed his intention, he must have changed his mind somewhere between Carlisle and Belfast. After disembarking at Belfast he headed straight for Duneight, in the townland of Blaris, a couple of miles from Annahilt. He went to the farm of a John Dawson, who he had grown up with, to enquire after a property to rent. Dawson's father had rented out properties for years, and John was gambling that his son was nowadays doing the same. He was right. Within two hours of meeting the farmer, John had taken on the tenancy of a two-roomed cottage at 15, Duneight, Blaris. It was stone built with a slate roof and three windows at the front, so had plenty of light inside. Most important, there was no sign of damp. Handily, it was next door to a grocery shop. A few bits of furniture and it could be very comfortable, he thought, as soon as it's in shape I'll maybe see what I can find out about Liza Jane. It turned out that he wouldn't have far to look for her. In fact he wouldn't have to look for her at all. News, any piece of news, spreads like wildfire in the countryside. Word was soon out and about that John Adams of Annahilt was home after 20-odd years in the army, spent "fighting in all sorts of places roun' the world".

One afternoon, slightly less than a year after he moved into the cottage, there was a knock at the door, and when he opened it a young woman was standing there. She said simply, "My name's Eliza Jane. Are you John Adams? My father?" Taken aback, all he could think to say was, "I am indeed. Come in. Come in. I was going to try and find you, myself." He beckoned her into the house. "Now let me look at you," said John, taking her two hands and stepping back, while trying not to look directly at the most obvious thing about her, she was heavily pregnant. If John Adams thought his life was complicated already, it was about to become even more so. Not only would he soon be a grandfather, he discovered that he already was one. How am I going to break this to the boys, he thought.

Eliza Jane was around 5 feet 1 inch tall, with hazel eyes and sandy hair. She was living in Newtownards, as it turned out, about 20 miles away. A neighbour had chanced to mention to her a few months back that a John Adams from Annahilt direction was home after many years in the army, and asked if he was maybe a relative. Eliza Jane had taken until now to pluck up the courage to visit him. She had a son, James, who she had left at home with her Aunt Martha. James was registered as having been born on July 15, 1872 in Newtownards district. His father was named in the registration as (yet another) James Sturgeon, and he and Eliza Jane are recorded as husband and wife, her maiden name being noted as Adams. *(4)* Samuel, the unborn child she was carrying when she met John, would be born a few months later, on July 13 1877, also in Newtownards. No father would named on his birth registration, and the mother had by this time reverted to her (maiden) Adams surname. Eliza Jane's Aunt Martha (McClean) was recorded as having been present at the birth. *(5)*

The same would be true of another son, Henry, born at Ballylesson, between Lisburn and Comber, on April 07, 1885. Except this time Aunt Martha wasn't present at the birth, and, whether due to a clerical error or another minor deception on Eliza Jane's part, the surname of the mother is registered as Adamson. *(6)* All three children were raised with the surname Sturgeon, and Eliza Jane would for many years be documented as a widow. Whether she and the James Sturgeon registered as her husband at her first son's birth were ever married is debatable. There is no record of any such marriage. Nor is there any record of the death that would have rendered Eliza Jane the widow that she later claimed to be. Against that, present at the death of her mother, Eliza Jane Sturgeon, at the mother's home in Ballylesson on January 08, 1873, was a James Sturgeon, who is registered as an "occupier" of the house. This may well have been Eliza Jane Adams' husband, or at least the person that was claimed to be her husband on the registration of her first child. It could not have been her stepfather of the same name, or he would have been described as the "husband" of the deceased rather than an "occupier" of the same house. *(7)*

It would be all too easy, from a modern perspective, to moralise and be judgemental in respect of Eliza Jane: to question her "self-respect" or supposed lack thereof. To do so would be wrong, on many levels. There is no doubting that self-respect is a wonderful thing - if you can afford it. To provide some perspective: the ordinary people of Ireland, as with those in Britain, were desperately poor at the time of Eliza Jane. In that respect at least, not much had changed since John had left to join the army. There were no governmental or social safety nets in place to provide monetary or any other kind of assistance, and few if any legal protections against exploitation by employers, landlords and others. A person could be sacked from a job and/or thrown out of their home on a whim. If for whatever reason someone was unemployed or unemployable, without the help of an extended family they and their immediate dependents might easily starve. If someone was sick and could not afford proper medical care their only resort was to pray and hope for the best. It was the women and, by extension, their children, who bore the brunt of the poverty and deprivation. Almost invariably, a woman will stick by and try to fend for her immediate family - be they children, parents or siblings - whatever the circumstances. To put it at its kindest, the same cannot always be said of a man. (Indeed, a less sympathetic interpretation of John's (non-)actions in respect of his daughter might conclude that he was guilty of abandonment.) Eliza Jane did whatever she felt she had to in order that she and her children could survive. If she does not appear to have had an awful lot of self-respect, that's because it was a luxury she simply could not afford. *(8)*

As a courtesy, John asked after Eliza Jane's mother, and learned of her death from bronchitis a few years back. *(9)*

John then found himself, or imagined he did, having to explain why he had not been around for her childhood. He didn't get very far before Eliza Jane looked at him with a raised eyebrow and said, "No need to explain". And nor was there. She didn't need to be told how a man comes to leave a woman who is pregnant with his child. John told her about Sarah, and about William and Jack. Though he didn't tell her of Sarah's ethnicity, or why the boys were in England, only that they were there for their schooling. Eliza Jane expressed her condolences regarding Sarah but was delighted to hear of William and Jack, "Oh, I have two wee brothers, do I. That's great news. Did you tell them about me, John." "Of course, I did," he replied, "And they're delighted."

Eliza Jane was no fool, "I'm sure they weren't too happy at all. It would have been some shock for them. Listen, I'd love to get to know them, but if it's going to cause problems, then let's just leave sleeping dogs lie." "Absolutely not," said John, "As soon as they come to Ireland they'll be meeting their sister. I'm sure they'll love you." "I won't hold you to that," she replied with a smile, "Do William and Jack look like you?" "No, not at all," he laughed, "They're both dark-haired and brown-eyed like their mother." She smiled, "They don't look like me either, then. My mother always told me I was the spit of you." "Oh you're an Adams all right," said John, while thinking to himself, 'I'm sure that didn't sit too well with Mr. Sturgeon'.

John had feared two things about meeting Liza Jane. One, that maybe she was embittered and would want them to meet only to berate him for abandoning her. And two, that he simply wouldn't like her as a person. He needn't have worried on either count. She showed no resentment towards him at all, and he liked her a lot. In fact they got along like a house on fire. She told him that she worked occassionally as a housekeeper. But that type of work was scarce, so sometimes she helped her aunt Martha, who took in people's clothes for sewing. From late autumn every year there was no scarcity of farmers looking for people to gather potatoes, so she'd often go "purta hoakin' for the farmers'".

"I remember your Aunt Martha as a wee girl," John told her over a cup of tea, "And she was a right wee divil. She used to call me Adam's Apple and ask why I hadn't brought Eve along with me. And she'd shout after your mother and me, 'our Eliza, surely you can git better than that ugly baste'." Eliza Jane was in stitches at the thought of it: "And now the same woman would cut the backside off a child for behaving like that." "And she never married?" Asked John, surprised at the news, "She was a good-looking youngster, too." "She's still good-looking," said Eliza Jane, "The best-looking one out of the McCleans. But she never had any interest in getting married. And it's not as if there was any shortage of offers, mind. But no, 'there'll be no man'll own me' she would say." John smiled, "That sounds like Martha, all right. Fair play to her." Eliza Jane became serious for a second, "She's been good to me, John. More of a mother than her sister ever was, if I'm honest." Eliza Jane pointed to her belly, "She took me in when I'd nowhere to go. Yes, I'd have to do some searching to find somebody as good as Martha McClean, that's for sure."

They chatted about John's time in the army, where he'd been and what he'd seen. He told her what winter was like in Crimea, "I'll put it this way, the coldest Irish winter's day that you can possibly imagine, would be a mild one in Crimea." He told her about eating rats, but she flatly refused to believe him. He still found it hard to believe, himself. The story of the flying fish was greeted with a similar degree of scepticism, "Well now, I'll have to watch out for them boyos the next time I'm near the Lagan or the Ravarnette River," she laughed.

The father and daughter really enjoyed one another's company. They were as relaxed and comfortable as if they had been friends for years. She was captivated by his descriptions of India. The food, the colours, the people and their religions, the animals, the heat, the rains, and the smells of spices. "You mean to tell me that an elephant, tame as a dog, was lifting tree trunks and setting them down just where the man wanted it to?" she marvelled. "Yes, gentle as lambs they were. And all yer man had to do was tap it on the ear with his stick and it knew what he wanted," explained John. "Oh, I'd love to go somewhere like that," she said longingly, "Somewhere far, far away from this place." It reminded him of how he'd felt all those years ago. The yearning to escape that was so intense his chest would ache. "How are you fixed at Newtownards?" John asked her. Then nodding at her belly, "There's aways a place for you and the youngsters here, you know. You've only got to say the word, and the door's open to you." "Ah it's grand, John," his daughter replied, "As long as I have Martha, I'm fine. But thanks for the offer, it's much appreciated. I might just have to take you up on it some day." "You're always welcome here, Eliza. I've got my army pension and I do bits and pieces of work for the farmers around here, so don't worry about the money. There'll always be room for you and the wee'uns in any house of mine," he assured her. Eliza Jane stayed the night at her father's house, and set off to walk back to Newtownards in the mid-morning of the next day.

At the same time as John was first meeting Eliza Jane, in late March 1877, 11-year-old William was preparing himself, mentally at least, for leaving school. His last day would be in July of that year, when the school broke up for the summer. He was fortunate that his birthday fell in August, or he would have had to leave the previous year. The same would apply to Jack, another August baby, when his turn came.

Whatever else about Long Sutton primary school, excepting those they too readily gave up on, the teachers did try to cram as much learning as possible into the pupils in the few years they had with them. At most, a working-class child would spend six years at school. And there was no guarantee that the teachers would have even that short length of time with them. A parent could pull their child from school at any time. And often did, to put them to work supplementing the household income. The teachers tried to engender a thirst for learning in their young charges: to excite an inquisitiveness that would hopefully lead to a lifetime's pursuit of knowledge. William and Jack could read and write to a relatively high standard before they were 10-years-old. And, by the same age, they were more than proficient in arithmetic. Every so often a teacher would set aside an afternoon for a lesson on history and geography (i.e. a paean to the British Empire). There were two classrooms at the school, each holding three classes. Each classroom had one teacher, who would flit between the classes adjusting her lessons to suit the differing age groups. Miss Copeland took the junior classes and Mrs Wells the seniors. Master Parsons dealt mainly with all aspects of the school's administration, as well as the punishments, and would sometimes take a keen interest in the tutoring of a child of a notable local resident. He also delivered the occasional history/geography lesson.

One morning, Mrs Wells announced to her classroom that Master Parsons would be giving a lesson that afternoon. And sure enough, when the seniors returned from their lunch break Parsons was waiting for them, standing bolt upright at the front of the room, legs apart with hands clasped behind his back. Sticking out slightly from behind him, at a 45 degree angle to his right leg, was the end of a bamboo cane, to be used as a pointer on the large map of the world that he had unfurled on the wall at the front of the room, or a weapon if the opportunity arose. More than half of the countries on the map were coloured pink to indicate that they belonged to the British empire. The rest of the world might as well have not have existed, as far as Parsons was concerned. He only ever dealt with pink-coloured countries in his history cum geography lessons. He would describe how Britain had, in the case of an African nation, for instance, brought civilisation and Christianity to "the savage natives". With the likes of Australia or New Zealand, he would talk of how "we" conquered innumerable natural hazards to make these erstwhile vast, inhospitable and "empty" lands habitable and productive. His British colonial history was littered with seafaring heroes like Captain Cook, Francis Drake and Sir Walter Raleigh.

The sub-text to everything that Parsons taught, and what he sometimes more or less openly stated, was that black and brown people were inferior in every way to white people – in intellect, culture, behaviours, and so on. They were humans, of course, but only just. The idea that they might "own" the lands they occupied was so ludicrous as to not even enter a sane person's thinking. It would be like considering a kangaroo or a tiger or a fox to be the rightful owner of the lands upon which it lived and roamed. It was an act of Christian benevolence on the part of white people to travel to these far-off lands to deliver a degree of civilisation to the natives. According to Parson's worldview, one that he shared with the vast majority of fellow British citizens from every walk of life, was that not all white people were equal. British people were superior to "foreigners" of whatever colour, of course – made clear by the propensity of large pink splodges on the world map, and the long list of battles in which they had been victorious. (The occasional loss on a battlefield was invariably put down to a relatively tiny British force refusing to concede to an enemy, despite being hopelessly outnumbered. Either that, or as the result of some heinous subterfuge on the part of a foreign nation.) But neither was it the case that all British people were equal. In descending order of merit, the Welsh, Scots, and Irish were British too, but this was largely down to them having the good fortune to live in close proximity to England. Sitting alone atop the world pyramid of humanity was the Englishman, of course. There by God's will.

The children enjoyed Master Parsons' classes. No effort was required on their part. All they had to do was behave and look interested. And, to be fair, the vast majority of them were genuinely interested. What better antidote to being on the lowest rung of your country's social ladder than to be assured you were at least superior to every person born elsewhere in the world. They also found it exciting to listen to stories of far-off lands full of strange people and even stranger beasts, such as kangaroos and tigers. They would dream of visiting these places themselves when they were older. Of course, two of the pupils didn't have to wonder. They had been born in one such place. This led indirectly to an embarrassing moment on the day of Mrs Well's announcement, which served as a reminder to William and Jack that they must never drop their guard.

"Quiet," shouted Parsons, merely as a reflex introduction to his lesson, as there was already not a sound to be heard from the assembled children, "Today we're going to talk about the East Indies," he announced, pointing with his cane to India, as it then was, on the map. "Hands up anyone who can tell me something about the East Indies," safe in the knowledge that none of them knew anything about the place. Or so he thought. Jack couldn't resist. In fact he didn't have to resist anything, so delighted was he to hear his homeland mentioned he wanted to acknowledge the fact. His hand shot up. "Yes, Pope minor? What can you tell us about the East Indies?" enquired Parsons. "Please sir, me and my brother William were born there," said Jack, nodding across at William, who nodded back in agreement. "My brother William and I," Parsons corrected him, "Ah yes, Pope minor,

I'd forgotten that. I should have remembered our two little Indians, with your black hair and swarthy skin." The rest of the class began sniggering and laughing, while Jack and William turned bright red and squirmed in their seats. Parsons knew immediately that he had hit a raw nerve with the boys, and he might possibly have guessed what it was. To his credit he moved swiftly to rectify the situation. "That's only my little joke, Pope minor. Of course I remembered that you and your brother were born in the East Indies," he lied, "The sons of Sergeant Henry Pope, who is still out there serving our country and our empire with distinction. You both should be very proud of him. No, I meant did anyone know how Britain is helping to civilise the people of the East Indies." Jack and William breathed a sigh of relief. William mouthed "kutcha" at his brother, who had become complacent. Neither of them would make a similar mistake again.

In July of 1877, William left school and went to work with Aunt Josie's husband, Sam, on a local farm. He was one month short of his 12th birthday. On account of his youth, the farmer, Mr Robinson, set William lightish tasks at the beginning. As his first job, he gave him a large wooden wheelbarrow and directed him to a meadow to collect cow-pats, to be added to a dung heap in the main farmyard. The barrow was tall and heavy, obviously not designed for use by a young boy, and at first William had to stand on his tip-toes to raise its shanks the tiniest bit off the ground. But he couldn't possibly do the job on tip-toes, so had to move his hands further down the shafts, closer to the body of the barrow, to get enough traction to lift it clear. But this, of course, significantly reduced the leverage and made the barrow feel heavier still. As he was wrestling with the wheelbarrow, and becoming increasingly embarrassed that he was failing dismally in the first job he had been set, laughter rang out from across the yard behind him. He turned, red-faced, to see that Mr Robinson and Sam were standing watching him. "Just our little joke, young William," Sam called out to him, "That fella's too big for you. Let's see if we can get you another one. His baby brother, perhaps." Sam motioned for William to follow him, and took him into a shed where another, much smaller, wheelbarrow sat. "There you are, young William. This fella's more your size," said Sam, and handed William a large wooden shovel to go with the barrow, "You'll need this too, for lifting the cow-pat."

Over the next year, William learned to weed, thin and harvest turnips, carrots, cabbage and parsnips. All of which was backbreaking work. The weeding and thinning of the vegetables would often be done under a hot Somerset sun. Their harvesting, more backbreaking still, was almost invariably carried out in heavy frost or rain, and sometimes even snow. From early autumn onwards, he gathered drill after drill of potatoes that Sam had dug up with a fork, until he dreaded bending down because it hurt his back so much. When he managed to do that, he would dread straightening up again because it hurt his back even more. He learned to gather into rows and then frequently turn the long grass that Sam had cut with a scythe. After a few days, when the sun had done its job, Sam taught him how to stack the resulting hay so that it wouldn't overheat and start to rot. And so it went on, day after day, week after week of backbreaking work. If he wasn't shovelling, he was lifting, or carrying, or sweeping, or dragging. He would do this six days a week, with Sunday off, arriving home to Nanna's each evening dirty and exhausted. Every Saturday, when they had finished for the day, Mr Robinson would hand him a shiny half-crown (12.5p) for his wages, two shillings (10p) of which he would give to Nanna towards his upkeep and the other sixpence he would keep for himself.

William hated farming. He hated it in his heart. Except, that is, for one aspect of it. He adored the horses. Robinson had two shire mares and a two-year-old gelding. Every morning, as soon as he arrived at the farm, William would call into the stables to greet them. He loved their power and grace, their gentleness. And how they would nuzzle his neck as he chatted to them. He would brush them down, combing their manes and tails until they were glistening, and feed them oats from his open outstretched hand. And the horses seemed to love William too. He had a way with them. He was too young and inexperienced to work horses himself, but he would help Sam harness one or both of the mares to a cart or a plough whenever the occasion arose. After their work was done, he would unharness them again, check their feet for stones, wash them down, and lead them back to the stables to be combed and fed. William had decided what he wanted to do with his life. Work with horses.

Eliza Jane called again to see John, in early June of 1877, and this time she brought her son, James, and Aunt Martha with her. "So this is my grandson," exclaimed John upon opening his door to them, "And how are you James?" "I'm fine, thank you, sir," replied James, as John was bending down to pick him up. "None of this "sir" nonsense, now," chided John, good-naturedly, "You'll call me granda. For that's what I am, your granda." He and Martha greeted one another like old friends. He had remembered her as a mischievous, fun-loving youngster of about 12-years-old. Now, standing before him was a woman who looked world-weary, aged beyond her years. She was some 12 years younger than John, but looked at least as old as his 47 years. "How are you keeping, Martha," asked John, "It's been a long time." "It has indeed been a long time, John," she answered, "I'm doing all right, thanks. Getting by, as they say. And what about yourself? Are you settling back into life at home again?" And so the small talk continued. Them chatting about times past, and characters long gone whose various antics had been the talk of the country. John noticed how James acted around Martha, like how a grandson would behave around his favourite granny. Those small interactions between woman and child confirmed everything that Eliza Jane had said about Martha, and how good she had been when his daughter had needed someone. At one point, as Eliza Jane was leaving the front room to use the privy, Martha nodded after her and said to John, "I can't tell you how happy she's been to have found you, John. She talks about little else these days." And then, in a mock angry voice, "And tell her no more of them stories of yours. If I hear flying fish mentioned again, I'll scream." "And I'm delighted to have found her, Martha," he assured her, then laughing, "And no more stories, I promise." Martha did become serious for a moment, "And don't judge her too harshly, John. She's had a hard life, believe me. But the same wee girl has a heart of gold." "She takes after her Aunt Martha, then," said John, and they both smiled. "Don't worry, Martha. She's my daughter, and I already love her like a daughter."

The following month, on July 13 1877, Eliza Jane gave birth to another son, Samuel, in Newtownards. Her aunt Martha was present at the birth. It was clear from the outset that something was wrong with Samuel, but the precise nature of the problem wasn't obvious. It had been a very difficult birth, and the hope was that Samuel would soon recover from his ordeal. The hope was in vain. Samuel had been deprived of oxygen for too long in the birth canal and had suffered permanent brain damage. One of the consequences of this was he had been left blind. Another was that his mental and emotional development would never extend beyond that of an average six- or seven-year-old.

John didn't hear about Samuel until mid-September, more than two months after the child had been born. He was chopping wood one day, replenishing his supply for the winter, when he glanced up and saw in the distance a woman walking along the road in the direction of his house. Nothing unusual in that. Until he glanced up again after a few minutes and realised it was Martha. That Eliza Jane wasn't with her told him something must be wrong. Before Martha had got within 50 yards of him he called out to her, "Hiya Martha, what brings you to these parts on your own? Nothing's wrong, I hope." Martha's reply did nothing to ease his concerns, "Hiya, John. I'll speak to you in a minute, when I get off my feet." When they had sat down with a cup of tea, Martha explained about Samuel, "I never witnessed anything like it, John. The baby got stuck, and she was in labour for nigh on 36 hours. For a while I really thought we were going to lose them both. How that child survived at all is beyond me." John shook his head, he thought this was even worse than losing a child, "Good God, that's all she needs." "Well, the wee girl's distraught, obviously. But she's determined to bring the child up as best she can, John. There's no turning her on that," Martha told him. "And I'll be there to help her in every way I can," she declared. "I know you will, Martha," said John, "I know you will."

They sat in silence for a while, then John said, "I can see there's something else bothering you, Martha. Do you want to tell me what it is? If it's none of my business, that's fine. But if there's anything you need to tell me, then don't be shy about saying it." Martha looked at him, then began to speak, "I have no right to be saying this to you, John Adams, but I'll not rest until I do. Eliza Jane has me, and I swear she always will, until the day they lower me into the grave. But I'm getting no younger, John, and I'm feeling it. What happens to her when I go? Who'll look after her and the wee'uns then?" "I will, of course," replied John, "Who else do you think would look after her?" "You're no spring chicken yourself, John, if you don't mind me saying so," said Martha, without the slightest hint of humour, "So God only knows which one of us will go first. But, leaving that aside, will you make me a solemn promise? Will you swear to me that if I go first you'll look after Liza Jane and the wee'uns? Now don't swear to me if you don't mean it, John. I'd rather know the truth, whatever it is, than be comforted with a lie. And don't forget, you've two sons who'll be needing looked after too, before very long." John felt quite emotional at the depth of Martha's love for and loyalty to her niece, his daughter. "Martha, I swear to you, with God as my witness, that I will always look after Liza Jane and the wee'uns. You need never trouble yourself on that front again. I have never thanked you properly for all that you've done for her. But I'm thanking you now. It's shame on me that you had to do it. But thank God you did. I don't know what would have become of her if you hadn't been there." "Thank you, John," said Martha, "I'll sleep easier tonight."

It was February 1878 before John met his new grandson, when Eliza Jane and Martha brought him and young James to the house one cold frosty day. "That's not a great day to be travelling," he ventured, at a loss for something else to say. Truth is, John was embarrassed. He didn't how he should react to Samuel. Should he congratulate Eliza

Jane on the birth of her son, admire and coo over him, and generally act as though there was nothing wrong with the child? Or should he offer condolences to his daughter on her not having been delivered of a healthy normal baby? There must surely be a position between those two extremes, but he couldn't think of it. Eliza Jane relieved him of his discomfort. As she unwrapped Samuel from her shawl, she said, "He'll need special looking after, John. And while me and Martha are alive, he'll always have it." And with that she gazed down at her son and stroked his face lovingly with a finger. "Yes, he's a special child indeed," said a relieved John, and held out his arms towards her, "Here, let me hold my special grandson." Martha grabbed James and pulled him to her, "And let's not forget our other special child," she said. Not for the first time in his life, John Adams marvelled at the wisdom of women.

In July of 1878, Jack left school and went to work with his brother and Sam on Robinson's farm. William's hatred of farming paled in comparison to what Jack felt about his new life. He despised every second of it. Unlike William, he didn't even have the consolation of the horses to fall back upon. He liked the horses well enough. And they took to him as easily as they had to William. But that was as far as it went. It wouldn't break his heart if he never saw another horse again. If nothing else, though, Jack had learned, not exactly patience, but the value at least of long-term planning since he had left India. He knuckled down to the job, and did the best he could, while keeping his mind firmly fixed on the ultimate goal.

William and Jack had been exchanging occasional letters with their father since they had last seen him in 1876. The boys kept John updated on Nanna and Aunt Josie, and told him about leaving school and how much they disliked working on the farm. Having worked on and around farms all of his young life, and detested it, he was in full sympathy with them. But he wasn't prepared to put that on paper, for fear of further unsettling them in their jobs. Instead he encouraged them to "stick at it" until something better came along. John would slip little references to Eliza Jane into his letters. Not much, at first. Just a mention here and there that she had called to see him. Gradually he began to describe what she was like as a person, how nice she was. Then he began to include "Eliza Jane sends her regards to both of you" and would mention how she was "really looking forward to meeting you". As John had intended, this sparked a discussion on Eliza Jane between William and Jack, and, as he hoped it would, their inquisitiveness got the better of them. "She sounds nice," remarked William one day, after they had read John's latest letter. "Yes, she does," agreed Jack, "And none of this is her fault. She didn't ask to be born." "Would you like to meet her some time? Just to see what she's really like," continued William. "I don't know. Would you?" countered Jack. "Yes, I might. Some time. It would do no harm, I suppose," replied William. "I wonder if he ever told Mama about Eliza Jane," said Jack, "I wouldn't want to meet her if Mama didn't know about her. It wouldn't be right." "Yes, I see what you mean," agreed William, "Let's ask him." And so they did, in a letter written and sent that very day. John wrote back, "I never kept any secrets from your Mama. I told her about Eliza Jane soon after we met, and then again before we were married. She understood. Her very words were, we both had lives before we met and what is done cannot be changed. Your Mama said she was looking forward to meeting Eliza Jane when we all went to live in Ireland. I never told you boys about Eliza Jane because you were far too young, but your Mama and me were always going to tell you before my time in the army was up. Before we went home to Ireland. When you were old enough to understand."

John was being perfectly honest in what he wrote, and the boys instantly recognised that. It sounded exactly how their mother would have reacted. In fact they felt a little guilty that their initial reaction to Eliza Jane had been so different to that of their mother's. "I'm going to go to Ireland to stay with Pappa, and meet Eliza Jane," announced William after they had read the letter, "Will you come with me?" Jack thought for a moment or two, "Yes, but not for a while, William." Jack was in a quandary. He now had no objections to Eliza Jane, either her existence or the idea of meeting and getting to know her, but he was afraid of his long-term goal being put in jeopardy by a trip to Ireland. He sensed that he might become bogged down in a family situation there that would be hard to extract himself from. "All right," said William, "We won't mention anything to Pappa just yet. We'll go when you're ready." What was about to happen would push all thoughts of Ireland out of their minds for some time.

(1 JA's Army Attestation papers https://www.fold3.com
(2 Civil registration of births did not become compulsory in Ireland until 1864. But the year of birth can be calculated from later official records
(3 Copy of the registration of the marriage courtesy of the Irish General Register Office via www.irishgenealogy.ie
(4 (5 and (6 copy of the registration of the births courtesy of the Irish General Register Office via www.irishgenealogy.ie
(7 Copy of the registration of the death courtesy of the Irish General Register Office via www.irishgenealogy.ie

(8 'Now he looks round the shack where he lives with his wife, four children, parents, widowed aunt and other family members, and despairs: "I am having to choose between selling my daughters or all starving," he said'. From a report by Christina Lamb: "In my 35 years as a reporter, I have never seen anything of Afghanistan's magnitude": the Sunday Times, January 30, 2022, https://www.thetimes.co.uk/article/in-my-35-years-as-a-reporter-i-have-never-seen-anything-of-afghanistans-magnitude-rpsv8qlvv
(9 Copy of the registration of the death courtesy of the Irish General Register Office via www.irishgenealogy.ie

Top: *The British Crimea Medal, of which John Adams was a recipient*
Below: *Its Turkish (Ottoman) equivalent, which John also received*

Records of John's death; Jack's marriage to Lillie Farrell; Lillie's death; and the 1901 census showing William living with Eliza Jane and family at his late father's home in Duneight near Annahilt

Extracts from William's and Jack's army attestation papers (they joined under the surname Pope); Jack's comment upon his discharge, "Free after 12 years"; when he rejoined at the outbreak of the First World War it was under his proper name of Adams, albeit with "alias Pope" included

Mary (nee McMann/McMahon) and Jack pictured on their wedding day; a record of their marriage; and records of their deaths in, respectively, 1933 and 1944

Chapter 8

Nanna

Nanna had suffered for years from periodic bouts of asthma, or "chestiness" as she and the family referred to it, particularly during spring and winter. In October of 1878, when she again went down with chestiness, no one thought much of it.

Henry had been in touch recently, via a letter to Josie, to say that he was just about to enter his last year in the army, and should be posted home to England soon to see out his final eight or nine months. This news caused great excitement in the Pope household, of course, and was assumed to have triggered Nanna's illness. At the beginning, Nanna pushed on with her daily routine of housekeeping for the magistrate during the day, and seeing to every need of William and Jack when they arrived home from work in the evenings. But after a few days she had to take to her bed, hardly able to breath. Again, this was not unusual. Josie was used to stepping in for Nanna whenever a bout of chestiness struck, doing what she could at the magistrate's house and seeing to the boys while her mother rested. After a week or so, her mother would normally be up and about again. Not this time though.

As the days went by, rather than easing, Nanna's breathing became increasingly laboured. Her coughing fits occurred more often and were more severe than usually was the case. Josie had noticed too that the phlegm her mother coughed up was sometimes flecked with blood. She wanted to call a doctor, but her mother wouldn't hear tell of it. "No need to waste good money on a doctor, love," she gasped, "This'll pass soon. It always does." Between looking after Sam and the girls, doing her mother's housekeeping job, and seeing to Nanna and the boys, Josie was run ragged. Finally Sam put his foot down, "Can't keep this up, my dear. You're going to have to get the doctor for your mother. 'Else you're going to be in a sick bed yourself before too long." Josie agreed. There was still no sign of the illness easing. When the doctor appeared at her bedside, Nanna looked relieved to see him, despite her earlier protestations. She began trying to tell him how she was feeling, but he gently shushed her, "Don't try to speak now, Mrs Pope. You rest while I give you a quick examination." Josie had waited downstairs while the doctor attended to her mother. She had a pot of tea and some scones ready for him when he came down. He motioned for her to sit down, waved away the tea and scones, and then sat down himself, facing her, "I'm sorry Josie, but I'm as certain as makes no difference that your mother has consumption." Josie was every bit as stoic as her mother, and had half-expected the prognosis to be bad. Despite this, she couldn't hold back the tears. "Can she get through it, doctor?" she finally asked. The doctor shook his head, while saying, "One can never tell, Josie. But at your mother's age ... somewhere in her mid-70s ... I'd be very surprised. I'll leave you to chat with the family, and I'll call back again tomorrow morning. You should consider what you want to do and tell me then." Josie had no idea what he meant by "consider what you want to do". She looked quizzically at him, pondering how to phrase her query. But he pre-empted her, "I mean whether you want your mother to remain here or go into hospital, Josie." Josie didn't need a family meeting to decide the answer to that, but the finality inherent in his remark brought the enormity of the situation home to her. She started to cry again. "I know, Josie," said the doctor, "But your mother will be waiting for you upstairs, so best if she doesn't see you crying." Suddenly something struck Josie, "Does she know, doctor?" "Yes, I told her my diagnosis, Josie. I know your mother long enough to realise that she wouldn't want to be told anything but the truth." "Thank you, doctor," said Josie.

After he had left, Josie made her way slowly upstairs, mounting each step with dread. As she opened the door to the bedroom, she saw that her mother was lying watching for her. She motioned Josie over to her side. "Don't worry, my love. I've had long life, and two wonderful children to brighten the way," she whispered, "It had to come to an end sometime. Anyway, I've no intentions of going until your brother gets home." She tried to laugh at her last remark, but was taken by a fit of coughing. "Oh mam, I do love you," was all Josie could think to say. Then they sat quiet, hugging one another.

"How are we going to tell the boys?" Josie asked Sam later that evening. "There's only one way to tell them,' said Sam, "And that's come straight out with it. If we leave it and say nothing, then they're liable to guess anyway. Or worse, something might happen with your mum, and they would realise that we were expecting it all along." But they needn't have worried, Nanna had decided to tell the boys herself. The very next morning, as if she had overheard their conversation, Nanna said to Josie, "Best to prepare the boys. But don't you go worrying about that, Josie. I'll tell them myself this evening." That night, when William and Jack were seated at her bedside, she gently raised the subject of her health, "The doctor was here the other day, and it seems I'm more sick than I thought I was." "How sick?" asked Jack. "Quite sick," replied Nanna. "But you're going to get better, Nanna, aren't you?" William asked. Nanna smiled comfortingly, and looked at them, "Maybe not, my loves. Maybe not. But don't you two go worrying your young heads about me. I'm not afraid to go. And when I do, I'll be taking a special message for a very special person with me." "First thing when I get up there," she continued, pointing to the ceiling, "I'll be telling your Mama how great her two boys are doing, and how much they love her. There now, won't that be nice?" They both nodded. And she put her arms around them, "Now don't you two be worrying about a thing. Your Nanna's not afraid, so there's no need for you to be. You'll always be well looked after. Aunt Josie will always be here for you. Henry will be home soon. And your father has a place waiting for you. So no need for you to worry at all, my loves."

Over the following weeks and months, Nanna's condition continued to deteriorate. Sometimes the change in her would be gradual and almost imperceptible, and at other times it was sudden and stark. She would be struck by bouts of coughing or high-temperature sweats, and all the while the weight dropped off her, until she looked tiny and skeletal in the bed. But still she hung on, refusing to die. At last, one early afternoon in early February 1879, Henry Pope stepped through the door of his mother's house in Long Sutton. It was the first time he had done so in more than 20 years. Josie was there to greet her brother. She had been writing to him, so he was well aware of their mother's illness and the prognosis.

Josie opened the door to her mother's bedroom and, from behind a beaming smile, said simply, "Mother, you have a visitor." She then stepped aside and Henry strode past her, into the room, and over to his mother's bed. Nanna had hardly the energy any more to raise her head from the pillow. She turned to face her visitor, assuming it was the doctor. Then she smiled in recognition, "Oh, my son, my son," she kept saying, the tears running down her face. Henry barely left his mother's bedside over the next five days. He sat chatting with her when she was awake, and held her hand while she slept. In the early hours of the morning of the sixth day after he arrived home, she passed away peacefully in her sleep. As good as her word, Mrs Pope had refused to succumb to her illness before she laid eyes on her son again.

After Nanna's passing, William and Jack were as upset as the other members of the Pope household but, importantly, not worryingly so. Perhaps it was the little chat that Nanna had had with them about her illness, or perhaps they took comfort from the formal goodbye afforded by a funeral. Or maybe they had become accustomed to saying goodbye to people they loved. Whatever the reason, much to everyone's relief, most especially Josie's, the boys appeared not to be overly affected by what had happened. Within a few weeks of the funeral, everything had returned to as close to normal as Josie and Henry could manage.

From his savings, and in anticipation of his army pension and termination payment, Henry paid a year's rent in advance on Nanna's house. He intended to live there after he had finished with the army, in eight months time (October 1879). The boys, now aged thirteen and eleven, continued to live at the house and paid for their upkeep as usual, except now they gave the money to Josie. She continued to flit between her own house and her mother's, waking the boys in the mornings and seeing them off to work, cooking their meals and doing their laundry. These arrangements would last until Henry came home for good.

When John heard of Mrs Pope's death he was deeply saddened, of course. But his thoughts turned, naturally enough, to William and Jack. What would this mean for them? Would they now, at last, be ready to come to Ireland? What if they do decide to come to Ireland? He hadn't yet told them of Eliza Jane's children, and, given their reaction to learning about the existence of a sister, he dreaded to think how they would respond to being told they had two nephews. He was relieved when letters from his sons subsequent to Mrs Pope's passing made no mention of them joining him in Ireland. If anything, the tenor of the letters suggested that the boys had every intention of staying in Somerset for the foreseeable future. He felt guilty at his sense of relief, but there was no denying it. Nor was there any denying that his relationship with Eliza Jane and her children had developed far beyond what he had imagined it might. At the outset, he had been driven largely by guilt for abandoning her, and the belated sense of parental responsibility which came along with that (plus, if he was honest with himself, a degree of inquisitiveness). But he had grown to love her as his daughter. He now considered Eliza Jane and the children, and even Martha to some extent, as family. Eliza Jane and her children had not supplanted William and Jack in his affections, but they had certainly joined them.

October came and went, yet Henry Pope did not return from the army. It would be another three months before he did so. He had been engaged in the training and reorganisation of English militia groups (equivalent to an army's reserves) and, when asked, had agreed to stay on for the extra few months. Finally, on January 20, 1880, he left the army and returned to Long Sutton to take up residence in his mother's old house. He had served 21 years and 333 days as a soldier; 16 years and five months of which were spent in India. *(1)*

It's fair to say that civilian life was going to take some getting used to for Henry Pope. In fact, he never did come to terms with it. All was fine at the beginning. He settled down at home with the boys, and the three of them got along as well as they ever had. In many respects, it was just like old times. Henry soon found employment, as a coachman in a livery stables, and William and Jack continued to work at Robinson's farm. But, beyond enjoying each other's company, none of them was happy, in any real sense. One winter's evening in late 1880, as they sat around the fire at home, Henry noticed that Jack was deep in thought, and, wondering if maybe there was a problem at work, asked, "Is something the matter, Jack?" "Yes, Henry," said Jack, matter-of-factly, "I want to go home to India." Henry was silent for a minute or two, then replied, "You and me both, lad. You and me, both." Despite their wishes, they were still in Long Sutton six months later.

On the night of April 3, 1881, a national census was conducted, and Henry (42), William (15) and John Henry (13) were duly recorded as the residents of a house at End of Kingsmoor, Long Sutton, Langport, Somerset. But they weren't the only residents. A Mary Ann Matilda Pope (25) is also recorded on the census as living there, and is described as Henry's wife. *(2)* The previous year, Henry had dropped some customers off in Yeovil, where Mary Ann was from. After having a bite to eat, he was waiting around, in the hope that someone would need a lift in the direction of Long Sutton, when a young woman came sauntering past. They exchanged smiles. And soon she came back again. She stopped this time, and they chatted for 10 minutes or so. Henry did indeed have company back to Long Sutton that day. Mary Ann travelled the 13 miles with him, and she had been there ever since. They were never married, nor did either of them intend for that to happen. Their relationship could best be described as one of mutual convenience. Mary Ann was not much older than the boys, or at least she was closer to them in age than she was to Henry, so she would chat with them as a young girl would. She was a decent good-natured young woman, always making jokes and clowning around. They liked her, and she liked them. Aunt Josie was not so keen on Mary Ann. Well, not her specifically, but the nature of the relationship that she and Henry had. Josie said nothing to Henry, but she made her disapproval clear. Her visits to the house suddenly became far less frequent after Mary Ann moved in. And when she did call, "to check that the boys are all right", her face would be like thunder, and any small talk would be directed exclusively to the boys.

There was no escape for Josie's husband, he had listen to it all, "He has that young trollop living there with him, and not a bit of shame in either of them. And in my mother's house, of all places. My mother's house! Can you believe it! The poor woman must be turning in her grave. And goodness knows what those two young boys must make of it all." Sam once made the mistake of seeming to offer extenuating circumstances in Henry's defence. "Well, I suppose that's the army for you," he said. Josie nearly exploded, "The army? The army? What in the name of goodness has the army got to do with anything? Is this what they teach them in the army? If it is, it's the first I ever heard of it. The army, indeed. So we're going to blame the army for this, are we? You make me wonder at times, Sam. You really do." It was a mistake Sam never made again.

As it happened, a few months after the census was taken, Mary Ann Matilda disappeared out of Henry's and the boys' lives just as suddenly as she had entered them. She decided to go back to Yeovil, tired, as she put it, of "this li'l old village where nothing ever happens". William and Jack were sad to see her go.

Henry's job as a coachman, essentially a taxi driver, could sometimes take him beyond the boundaries of Somerset. He had also retained his links with the army, or at least the militias, by hiring himself out to help train and organise men and design courses. This too would often take him to other parts of the country. He made numerous contacts and connections through these two lines of work. One contact in particular, Sergeant-Major Desmond Lynch, Commander of the 3rd Volunteer Battalion, The Royal West Surrey Regiment (The Queen's), helped shape the future for not only himself, but for William and Jack as well.

(3)

Encouraged by Nanna from the outset, both William and Jack had been saving money from their wages every week since they started working on the farm. Not very much, but always at least thruppence (1.25p), and sometimes as much as sixpence (2.5p). First Nanna and then Josie would keep the money for them, marking the amount each week in a little book set aside for the purpose. The boys could draw on their savings whenever they wished, usually for clothes or a birthday or Christmas presents. But they didn't squander money, and their savings had mounted up over the years they had been working. This was especially true where William was concerned, as he had started work two years before his brother.

In the April of 1882, William mentioned to Jack that he would like to use some of his savings to go over to Ireland to visit their father and asked him would he come along. Jack, who by this time had learned a little diplomacy, said, "I'd love to, William. But I'm sure old Robinson wouldn't let both of us off work at the same time. But you go over anyway. He'll be delighted to see you. You can explain why I couldn't come." After William had spoken to Henry and Josie, and was granted time off work by Mr Robinson, he sat down to write to his father.

John was delighted when he read of William's proposed visit. Here at last was a chance to start bringing his family together. He was disappointed that Jack wouldn't be coming, but relieved at the same time. He wanted to see his younger son as much as he wanted to see William. But he knew that building a relationship between the boys and Eliza Jane and her family would be much more difficult if Jack were around from the start. Best if William met Eliza Jane and her children on his own at first, and, if all went well, he could go back to Somerset and start laying the ground with Jack. John wrote back to the boys immediately, to say how much he was looking forward to seeing William and lamenting the fact that Jack wouldn't be with him. William replied just as promptly, telling John to expect him "sometime in July".

On the morning of July 09, 1882, William arrived in Belfast on the overnight boat from Liverpool. It was the first time, a month short of his 17th birthday, that he had set foot on Irish soil. William took a coach to Lisburn, and from there another one to Duneight. John, who had been staying close to home since the beginning of July, was weeding a bed of scallions at the back of his house when he heard the sound of a coach on the road. He rushed round to the front, to be there to greet his son. It had been six years since John had last saw William, and the picture he had of him in his mind was still that of a 10-year-old boy. He hardly recognised the young man that stepped down from the carriage and stood in front of him with arms outstretched. William, at just over 5 feet 4 inches tall, was now only two inches shorter than his father. "Pappa," said William, "It's so good to see you. You're looking well." John said nothing, and just took his son in his arms. He had waiting a long time for this meeting.

When they were seated in the house, William dutifully passed on best regards from Jack and Henry, and they engaged in some small talk around farming, the weather and one another's daily lives. Then John said what was on both of their minds, "I wish your mother and Jack were here. This is what I wanted for the four of us. It's what she always wanted. The four of us living together, our own wee family, here in Ireland. It wasn't too much to ask of life, was it? I still think about her all the time, you know. All the time." William spoke to his father, "I can still see her face, as clear as day, even though it was so many years ago now. And I can still hear her voice, chatting away to me and Jack in her mixture of languages?" Then he suddenly asked, "She was as nice a person as I remember her, Papa, wasn't she?" John smiled, "She was indeed, son. Every bit as nice. You couldn't have had a better mother. That day she took sick, the only thought she had was that you and Jack should be taken away from her in case you caught it. How is Jack? I mean, how is he really?" William thought for a minute, "Jack has never really accepted Mama dying, Papa. The unfairness of it. He's angry inside. And I think he's afraid. Afraid of ever being hurt like that again. But he's a good person, Papa. And he's smart. He manages fine. So don't worry about him too much. I look out for him. We look out for each other. We'll both be fine." John began to bring William up to speed on the sister he had yet to meet. He decided to jump in at the deep end, and borrowed Martha's "don't judge her too harshly" line to introduce the news of her two children and the lack of certainty around their paternity. To his relief, William just shrugged in response, as if to say "who cares". John described Liza Jane as best he could, and finished with, "She's a lovely person, William, you'll really like her." "She sounds lovely, Papa. I can't wait to meet her and the children," and, typical of William, he added, "She's my sister. And that's how I'll treat her." Then, almost as an afterthought, "Does she know about us, Papa? Does she know about Jack and me being half-Indian?" John looked him straight in the eye, "No son, I haven't told a sinner about you and Jack. Not even Eliza Jane. I'm certain she would never repeat it if I did tell her. But that's for you and your brother to decide." "I'm sure that's true, Papa, but I think the fewer people we tell, the better," said William, then he laughed, "So, I'll be William Adams here in Ireland, and William Pope back in Somerset." "I agree," said John, smiling inwardly, still thinking of Eliza Jane, who would hardly be unfamiliar with the idea of using different surnames when it suited. "Do you think Jack will come round to Eliza Jane and the boys?" John asked William. "Yes, I do," his son replied, "Jack has a good heart, but he likes to make up his mind on things in his own time, Papa. He's naturally suspicious of people, and he won't be rushed in his judgements. But he'll be fine in the end." "That sounds like an Adams, all right," laughed John. William frowned, "I don't think you're like that at all." "I take after my mother's side," declared John, and they both burst out laughing.

John sent word to Eliza Jane and Martha that William had arrived, and invited them to the house to meet him. The message was delivered by a mutual friend who happened to be going to Newtownards, so John couldn't afford to elaborate beyond the bare invitation. Eliza Jane was a bundle of nerves at the thought of meeting her younger brother for the first time. For a while, she had Martha tortured with her worries: "What if he doesn't like me?", "What if he's jealous of me and our father getting along so well?", "What if he doesn't take to the children?" On and on it went, until Martha had heard enough, "If he doesn't like you or the children, then he won't be worth getting to know. And the same applies if he's jealous of you and John. Let's wait and see if you like him, instead of getting yourself into a tizzy about him liking you." Martha was nervous herself, knowing what this meeting meant to Eliza Jane. But she wasn't going to show it.

On July 14, 1882, John and William were sitting sunning themselves outside the cottage at Duneight, when two specks appeared on the road in the far distance. "There's your sister and her aunt now, if I'm not mistaken," declared John. And as they got closer he added, "And they've got the two youngsters with them." When the little family reached the front gate, Eliza Jane didn't quite know how to greet William, so she did what came most naturally to her. Throwing open her arms she said, "Ah William, so I've got to meet you at last." William responded in kind, and as they hugged he said, "My goodness, Eliza Jane, but aren't you the picture of our father." Martha and John glanced at one another approvingly. This was just the kind of start they had hoped for.

They all sat outside in the sunshine, chatting a little awkwardly at times, while Eliza Jane nursed Samuel, and James played around their feet. He had already exhausted his "Uncle Willum" who had played with him most of the afternoon. During a lull in conversation, William reached out his arms towards Eliza Jane, "Here, let me hold my other nephew." "He's a wee bit...," Eliza Jane started to say, but William interrupted before she would finish, "I know. I know," and continued to reach for the child. As William sat rocking Samuel in his arms, chatting softly in baby-talk, and rubbing his cheek, the child lay contented, sometimes cooing back at him. Martha was astounded, "My God, John, that's the first time I've ever seen that child take to anyone except his mother. He won't even settle with me. I've never seen the likes of it." Later, when the children fell asleep, William said to Eliza Jane, "Right, big sister, how about you and me going for a walk." Eliza Jane stood and looked up at him, as though comparing their heights,"More like wee sister, but yes let's do that."

When they had gone, Martha turned to John, "He's a lovely young fella, John, he really is. Very handsome too. He doesn't look at all like yourself." John laughed, "Thanks, Martha." "No, I didn't mean that like it sounded. I meant he's so dark," she explained, "Is the other fella the same?" "If anything, he's even darker," said John, "They both take after their mother." They sat for a while in silence, then Martha said to him, "Listen, John, and hear me out before you say anything. I see how close you and William are. So I don't for a minute believe that you sat here all these years without him and his brother just so they could be educated in England. It's not as if we don't have any schools here in Ireland. And I can't help but notice that you and him change the subject any time the mother is mentioned. I don't want to know your business. I really don't. But I think I can guess why neither of you want to say too much. And I understand. You're right to keep it to yourselves. That's all I wanted to say." In reply, John said, "Thank you, Martha. I appreciate that." They sat for a few minutes more and then, to change the mood, Martha nodded in the direction of Eliza Jane and William who could be seen in the distance, strolling back from their walk arm in arm, "Now there's a sight that would gladden your heart," she said. John didn't answer, and she turned to see why. The old soldier was nodding in assent, tears on his cheeks. As they walked along the road, Eliza Jane asked William about Jack, "Do you think he'll take to me and the wee'uns as easily as you have, William." "Don't worry about Jack," he replied, "He's slower to warm to people than me, but he'll be fine. As soon as he gets to know you, he'll take to you the same as me. How could he not? I'm proud to have you as my sister, Eliza Jane, and so will he be. We're family." Eliza Jane hugged his arm in delight. Those words meant everything to a young woman who had suffered rejection, in one form or another, all of her life.

Eliza Jane and Martha had only intended staying the night at Duneight, but John and William wouldn't hear tell of them leaving the next day. "We'll squeeze everyone in somewhere," was John's answer to Martha's half-hearted claim that there wasn't enough room for them all. After another failed attempt at leaving the following day, they ended up staying for a week. When it did come time to return to Newtownards, goodbye tears were shed. But they were tears of joy. Less than a week later, on July 24, William bade his father farewell, before setting off for Belfast to catch the boat back to Liverpool. "Be sure and come over again soon, son. And make sure Jack comes with you next time," John shouted to William, as the coach got ready to leave. "I will, father. I will indeed," William shouted back. Late on the night of July 26, he arrived back in Long Sutton, where news awaited him.

Sergeant-Major Desmond Lynch of the 3rd Volunteer Battalion, The Royal West Surrey Regiment (The Queen's) was a retired soldier of some renown. He had joined the Queen's Royal Regiment as a boy soldier, and gradually worked his way up through the ranks, serving for many years in India and seeing action during the 2nd China War (1856 - 1860). He was awarded the Long Service and Good Conduct Medal, the Meritorious Service Medal and the Medal for The Second China War with bars for Peking 1860 and Taku Forts 1860.

Upon retirement from the regular army, Lynch joined the Royal Surrey Militia as an instructor. His word and opinion carried a lot of weight in military circles. He happened also to be an acquaintance of Henry Pope. When he took up his position as instructor of the Royal Surrey Militia, and ran a long-practiced eye over his new charges, Sergeant-Major Lynch knew immediately that he needed the help of a few dependable old sweats to whip these men and boys into some kind of acceptable military shape. He asked around and was pointed in the direction of retired Sergeant, now coachman, Alfred Henry Pope from Long Sutton in Somerset. A glance at Henry's army record was enough to tell Lynch that this was exactly the kind of (former) model soldier that he needed. Henry, who was already engaged in providing training to militias, jumped at the opportunity to work with Lynch. It would be wrong to say that Henry and Lynch became close friends. Old deeply-ingrained military customs, in particular with regard to ranks, do not so much die hard as never die at all. But the two did hit it off when they met, and grew to like and, more importantly, respect one another a great deal. Between them they soon had the Royal Surrey Militia looking and acting like what they were supposed to be, an army unit. Albeit one to be held in reserve. But both men were confident that if or when the Royal Surrey's were called into action, they would not fail the test.

Henry's work with the Royal Surrey's was drawing to a close, when Sergeant-Major Lynch asked him what he proposed doing next. "Well Sergeant-Major," Henry replied, "I suppose I've no other option but to go back to coach driving." "You know your talents are wasted doing that," said Lynch, "You should be training men full time." "Yes, I miss the army life, but at my age I'm afraid I've no other option, Sergeant-Major," Henry replied, with more feeling than he had intended. "Well, I don't know about that, Sergeant," declared Lynch, with a twinkle in his eye, "A man with your talents and commitment shouldn't be wasted. Would you be interested in doing some work in the colonies? Somewhere like Ceylon [now Sri Lanka], for example?" Henry's heart skipped a beat, "I certainly would, Sergeant-Major. I'd jump at the chance." "Leave it with me," said Lynch, "And I'll see what I can do." The Ceylon Volunteers was established on April 01, 1881, as a reserve force and local arm of the British Army. The new volunteer force was commanded by British officers, but its ranks were filled largely by local volunteers. It was, in effect, a Ceylonese version of the militias in Britain and Ireland. And, like the militias at home, it was in dire need of high calibre British ex-army soldiers to train the men. This is what Lynch had in mind for Henry. *(4)*

As promised, Lynch made a few enquiries, and when next he met Henry he put a proposal to him, "There's a job there waiting for you, Sergeant Pope, if you want it. If you decide to go, the British Army will pay your fare to Ceylon. They're eager for men like you. An ex-soldier with your experience and record of service. Though strictly speaking you'll be a civilian, you'll retain your rank as sergeant for the purposes of the training. What do you say?" Henry could have kissed Sergeant-Major Lynch, but settled for thanking him instead. "I have two sons to sort out first, Sergeant-Major. The poor lads, their mother passed away while we were in India. But once that's done, I'm ready to travel at the army's convenience." Lynch asked about the boys and immediately suggested a solution to that problem, "So they're interested in joining the army too, you say. Well, if they're anything like their father they'll be an asset to our military. Get them up here and into the militia, and we'll soon sort them out with jobs and somewhere to live." Henry was ecstatic. He had thought at his age any chance of him getting back into army life was long gone. Now that an opportunity had arisen, he just couldn't let it pass. He wouldn't let it pass.

Henry waited until William came home from Ireland, and then sat him and Jack down, explained everything and asked them what they thought. Jack was delighted at the thought of escaping the farm, and almost as happy at the prospect of joining the Royal Surrey militia. He would have been happier still if they could have gone to Ceylon with Henry, but he knew that wasn't a possibility. William said he would be sad to leave Josie and Sam, but thought this was a perfect chance for all of them. "Anyway," he said, "If me and Jack don't like Surrey, we can always go over to Ireland to live with father. But this Ceylon job is perfect for you, Henry. You must take it."

When Henry next met with Sergeant-Major Lynch, at Sloughton Barracks in Guildford, to make final arrangements for his departure to Ceylon, he had William and Jack with him. "Well now," said Lynch to the boys, "Your father is going to be leaving England soon, to serve his country again, so we need to decide what to do with you two. Tell me about yourselves." During the resulting conversation, Lynch learned that both could read and write, they hated farm work, they wanted to join the army, and William loved horses. "Right, all of that sounds good," said Lynch, when he thought he had heard enough, "If you want to go for a walk with your father here, and come back to me in an hour, we'll have another chat." He nodded in Henry's direction, "I should have something arranged by then, Sergeant Pope."

When Henry and the boys came back, Lynch had indeed "something arranged". If they agreed, William and Jack would be sworn into the Royal Surrey Militia immediately, though they would not report for duty until September 03. On the same date, William would begin work as a junior groom at Sloughton Barracks, helping tend to the horses of the regular army's Royal West Surrey Regiment at Sloughton Barracks. For this he would be paid three shillings a week.

Living accommodation for him and Jack would consist of a small room off to the side of the stables. He hadn't yet been able to arrange a job for Jack, but "had something in the works" and was waiting for word back from one of his militia men. He was confident that before long Jack would be working again too. Lynch looked at the boys, and then Henry, and back to the boys again, "So, what do you say?" They said 'yes', of course, and were duly sworn into the militia.

Henry accompanied the boys back to Long Sutton, where he stayed for three days before heading to Southampton on the first leg of his journey to Ceylon. The final parting was sad for Henry and the boys, but tinged with excitement at what lay ahead of them all. The old soldier was returning to a life that he loved, and his charges were about to leave one that they hated. Still, the leaving was far from easy. William and Jack were saying goodbye to a man who had not only saved their lives, but had provided them with new ones. He deserved all of the tearful thanks they bestowed upon him before he left. Leaving Aunt Josie, Sam and the family was particularly difficult for the boys. Like her mother before her, Josie had treated William and Jack as though they were her own sons. And they loved her almost like a mother. Tears flowed on all sides, hugs and kisses were delivered, and numerous promises to keep in touch were made before they boarded a coach on the first leg of their journey to Guildford. "There'll always be a home for you here. Never forget that," shouted Josie, just before the boys set off on the morning of September 02 1882, to begin a new phase in their lives. Neither of them would ever set foot in Somerset again.

Home

William and Jack settled easily into life at Sloughton Barracks. Living on an army base was all they had known for the first few years of their lives. It felt perfectly natural to them. William enjoyed working with the horses, and Henry was soon employed as a painter cum handyman around the barracks. They also liked being part of the militia, into which they were warmly welcomed by the existing members as "Sergeant Pope's sons" (which suggests that Henry had lost none of his talent for being able to maintain friendships with men under his command). Not that the militia took up much of the brothers' time. After an initial training period of around 60 days, and a 28-day period set aside each year for further training, the meetings and general activities of the militia were irregular. Still, thanks to Henry's training and Lynch's leadership, the Surreys had an air of soldierly professionalism about them that was comparable to their regular army counterparts. This garnered the militia and, most especially, Sergeant-Major Lynch lots of plaudits, but it worked against them in another respect. Many of the men enjoyed their first taste of army life so much that a steady stream of them kept leaving to join the regulars. William and Henry were no exceptions. Though they had always intended joining the army anyway, after a short time in the Surrey Militia they were chomping at the bit to do so. In June 1883, William suggested to Jack that they both apply for a transfer to the regulars. Much to his surprise, Jack was hesitant. "Let's wait a while," he said. "Why should we wait?" asked William, thinking Jack had maybe changed his mind, "You've always wanted to join the army." "I'd rather wait until I grow a bit taller," Jack told him, "But you go ahead without me." Jack had always been the shorter of the two. William, approaching his 18th birthday, was just short of 5ft - 5ins tall, and had been since he was 16 yrs-old. Jack, coming up to his 16th birthday, stood at just over 5ft - 1ins tall. Like most short males, he was sensitive about his height. And like many before and after him, he waited in his youth for a growth spurt that would never arrive.

Having been through so much together, relied upon and supported one another throughout their young lives, William and Jack were far closer than most siblings. They were best friends, and could trust one another completely. At first, the thought of them separating horrified William. Throughout the summer he would periodically raise the proposition that they should join the army together, but Jack wouldn't budge. What he did manage to do though, without being aware of it, was convince William to go ahead without him.

Jack had changed a lot. He was still given to fits of anger when he felt slighted, but these were now few and far between. In fact, he was happier at Sloughton than his brother had seen him in a long time. He enjoyed his new job, was an excellent soldier and had made many friends among both the army personnel at the barracks and other members of the militia. It gradually dawned on William that, not only would Jack be fine without him, it might actually do them both good to branch out on their own a little. After a final chat with his brother in August of 1883, William decided to take the plunge. He wanted to continue working with horses, and army friends at Sloughton recommended that he apply to the Commissariat and Transport Corps. This he duly did, and at Aldershot on September 07 1883 he enlisted as William Pope and was given the regimental number, 5001.

William's attestation details read as follows: Birthplace: Lucknow, Oude; Height: 5ft 4.75ins; Hair: dark brown; Eyes: dark brown; Vaccinated as an infant (which might help explain how he escaped the cholera outbreak at Peshawar); Trade: groom; Previous Service: 3rd Battalion West Surrey Militia. He cited as his father, "Barrack Sergeant Alfred H Pope, at Kandy Ceylon. *(5)*

John was delighted when he received word that William had joined the army. Though he thought it somewhat ironic that he chose the Commissariat. "Let's hope they've improved since Crimea," he thought.

Through no fault of his own, William's time in the army was short-lived. Only a few months after he joined, in November 1883, he spent eight days in hospital with anaemia. Much worse was to come. On June 25 1884, he was severely injured when kicked by a horse, suffering blows to the back of his head and left shoulder. A month later, on June 30, he was admitted to hospital, and spent 143 days there recovering from his injuries. But he never did fully recover. On January 08 1885, he was back in hospital for treatment to a large abscess on his back that had resulted from the wounds inflicted by the horse. His stay was 63 days, this time. But the horse had inflicted more lasting damage than a large abscess. William was diagnosed as suffering from epilepsy. On January 01 1887, he was transferred to the army reserve, and two years later was deemed medically unfit and discharged. William had spent 5 years and 124 days in the regular army. His attestation papers describe his conduct as "Exemplary".

In September 1884, Eliza Jane, Martha and the children paid one of their regular visits to John. As they sat chatting, he couldn't help but notice the atmosphere was slightly stilted. He knew they had something to tell him, and it wasn't good news if their demeanours were anything to go by. Finally, in an exasperated tone, Martha turned to Eliza Jane, "Well, are you going to tell him, or will I?" Eliza Jane looked at her father apologetically and, in a low voice, said, "I'm pregnant again." John burst out laughing in relief, "God, is that all it is. You had me worried there. Well, is there any chance of you having a wee girl this time." Eliza Jane hugged him, "Thank you, John. I promise, I'll do my best to have a wee girl." On April 07, 1885, Eliza Jane gave birth to a healthy baby, another boy. She named him Henry. When joining the army, William had given his exact age, "18 years and 1 month". His brother, however, was not always as precise about such matters. Throughout his life, Jack would be inclined to deduct a few years from his age if he felt it suited his purpose. And this was the case when, three months after William, Jack also joined the army. He travelled to London on February 29, 1884 (a Leap year) to undergo a medical and swear an oath of allegiance. On March 04, he formally enlisted in the Royal Field Artillery as John Henry Pope at Hilsea in Portsmouth and was given the regimental number, 41653. He did so as a "boy soldier", claiming his age to be 14yrs and 5 months (the recruiting sergeant may have suspected something, for he noted that Jack's age was "Physically Equivalent" to 15yrs and 6 months). His true age was, in fact, 16yrs and 7 months. His height was 5ft 1.25ins (it appears his long wait for a growth spurt would continue in the army); Eyes: brown; Hair: dark brown. He too claimed his father to be Barrack Sergeant Alfred H Pope currently in Colombo, Ceylon. *(6)*

Jack underwent some basic induction training - such as regimental history, cleanliness, discipline and drill - at Hilsea Barracks in Portsmouth. After a few months, he was moved to the Gunnery School at Shoeburyness in Essex to begin training in small arms, fieldcraft and the use of heavy artillery. Semi-curricular activities included literacy classes, and individual and team sports.

Jack's life, thus far, had seldom been without incident and drama. And during his military training it continued in the same vein. On February 26 1885, while he was at Shoeburyness, an explosion at the experimental ranges there killed seven members of staff. A Colonel Frank Lyon had come from Woolwich Arsenal to test some fuses he had developed that were considered too dangerous to be tested at his own base. (It seems strange that no one considered they might also be too dangerous to be tested at Shoeburyness.) As an ill-fitting fuse was being gently tapped into a shell by a Sergeant-Major Daykin there was a large explosion which killed or fatally injured the seven men, one of the latter was Colonel Lyon. Lyon lost both legs in the explosion and succumbed to his injuries the next day. *(7)*

After 21 months of training, Jack and his colleagues travelled to Portsmouth in early January 1886 and boarded an "Indian Troopship", the HMS Crocodile. There were five such purpose-built Indian troopships - Crocodile, Euphrates, Jumna, Malabar, and Serapis (though Serapis was later reassigned as a training ship) - each able to carry 1,200 passengers. They operated only during the "trooping season", from September to March, to avoid the extreme heat in India. As can be imagined, conditions on the ships were basic, with ventilation particularly bad. Another problem was the constant tension between soldiers and sailors, as a sailor's ditty from the time amply illustrates: "A messmate before a shipmate, a shipmate before a stranger, a stranger before a dog, but a dog before a soldier." Jack's journey appears to have gone without any incident of note, however, and after a four-week sailing, which took them through the Mediterranean, the Suez Canal, and across the Arabian Sea, they docked at Bombay (now Mumbai) harbour on February 04, 1886. On that day, Jack officially graduated from boy soldier to regular trooper. But that was the last thing on his mind as he leaned on the ship's railings looking out over Bombay, "Home at last," he muttered to himself, "Home at last."

Widower

John Adams was home, too. And there he would remain. Living out his final days at Duneight, a mere four miles from Annahilt where he had been born and raised and had been desperate to escape from in 1855. He had experienced or witnessed war, disease, famine, extreme depths of poverty, and racial and religious discrimination and injustices on his travels. Similar to what he had left behind in his home country, if truth be told. Except all on a much greater scale.

It seemed to him as though everything in his home district had changed, and yet nothing much had changed at all. Fields of purple flax flowers were still a common sight, but not as much as before. Or maybe it just seemed that way because he now enjoyed gazing across them. People no longer spoke of the United Irishmen, but they still went to the grave of Betsy Gray each year to lay flowers. There were very few people left that John had known previously, but many of their descendants remained. Including those of James Little, who continued to be ostracised. There was no longer famine, or exceptionally hard winters and summers, but money and food were still hard to come by for ordinary working people. Diet and sanitary conditions remained poor, and working environments had hardly improved at all since he left. Deaths from illness and disease were only slightly less common. It would still take very little to tip the scales from survival to catastrophe for a vast majority of the Irish people.

John had suffered personal tragedy with the loss of Sarah, but he was glad he had left Ireland. And he was equally glad to be home again. It was in Duneight that he and his two sons, William and Jack, and his daughter, Eliza Jane, were finally united.

He had no money concerns during the final years of his life. Records show that each month he collected his army pension of £1:00 in the nearby town of Lisburn. *(8)* This, and the money he had received at his army discharge, was more than he needed. He continued to do the occasional odd-job for a farmer if asked, but more often than not a bite or two of food would be payment enough.

John Adams died on January 11, 1897, aged 66 years. *(9)* The cause of his death is recorded as "Bronchitis for 3 months. Effusion of the brain, 4 days". William is named on the death certificate as the main witness to his father's death. John is described as, "Army pensioner. 55th Regiment". And under "Marital Status" Sarah is remembered and properly recognised with one simple but powerful word: "Widower".

First name(s)	John
Last name	Adams
Service number	1477
Rank	Private
Unit or Regiment	55th (Westmorland) Regiment of Foot
HQ location	Chukrata, India

(1 Army Attestation papers of Alfred Henry Pope, https://www.fold3.com
(2 From the UK National Census of 1881, www.search.findmypast.co.uk
(3 Sergeant-Major Desmond Lynch via queensroyalsurreys.org.uk
(4 Shortage of troops in Ceylon and calls for old soldiers to apply as trainers were carried in various newspapers (Colonies and India on April 01, 1881; Indian Daily News on April 04, 1881; The Graphic on April 19, 1884 et al), www.search.findmypast.co.uk
(5 Army Attestation papers of William Pope alias Adams, https://www.fold3.com
(6 Army Attestation papers of John Henry Pope alias Adams, https://www.fold3.com
(7 The Southend Standard, 27 February, 6 March and 13 March 1885, www.search.findmypast.co.uk
(8 From the Permanent Chelsea Pensioners, Belfast Pension District Advice List, https://www.fold3.com
(9 Copy of death certificate courtesy of the Public Records Office Northern Ireland (PRONI), https://www.nidirect.gov.uk/campaigns/public-record-office-northern-ireland-proni

"Purtie hokin" [potato gathering] as it would have been for Eliza Jane

Epilogue

John Henry "Jack" Adams

Jack served in the Royal Artillery for 12 years and 90 days. Some 10 years and 30 days of that period were spent in India. A year before he was due to be discharged he re-engaged (on April 23, 1895) to complete 21 years of service. But for some reason he changed his mind. Typical of his sometimes fiery nature, Jack is quoted on his attestation papers as remarking at his discharge, on June 02, 1896, "Free after 12 years". The papers name him as "John Henry Pope".

After leaving the army, Jack moved to Belfast and, just as his brother William had done before him, he reverted to his true surname of Adams. Jack was a five-year-old child when he had last seen his father, and they were only re-united when he was an adult. They did not have much time to get to know one another again and rebuild their relationship, as John died a mere seven months after Jack arrived in Ireland. There is nothing to suggest that Jack and Eliza Jane didn't hit it off when they met. But, unlike in the case of William, nor is there much to suggest that they did. Eliza Jane and Jack would have been strangers to one another, and Jack was never as placid or easy-going as his brother.

On January 04, 1898, Jack and Lillie Farrell were married at the Church of St Aidan in Belfast. *(1)* Lillie died of tuberculosis on February 12, 1900, a little over two years after the marriage. *(2)* In 1901, Jack, a widower, was living alone at Bentham Street in Belfast. *(3)*

By 1911, he was living at Fortingale Street in Belfast with his second wife, Mary, this author's grandmother, and their three children. *(4)* Another child, my father Ernest, would be born at Fortingale Street on April 13, 1911, shortly before the family moved to the Lisburn area. Jack and Mary had been married at Christ Church, Belfast on April 02, 1904. Mary (nee McMann/McMahon), whose parents were from the south Down and north Louth areas, had been born and raised in Belfast. *(5)*

In January 1914, the family was living at 72 Hillhall Road, Lisburn. By then, Jack had joined the Lisburn District of the South Antrim Division of Edward Carson's Ulster Volunteer Force. *(6)* On September 02 of the same year, only weeks after the outbreak of the First World War, he rejoined the British Army, signing on to the Royal Irish Rifles. He did so under his own name, John Henry Adams (albeit with "alias Pope" added for clarification). *(7)*

One can only speculate on why Jack decided to dispense with the Pope pseudonym on official army papers. Perhaps at the time of enlisting in the Royal Irish Rifles he was required to provide proof of birth and birthplace. Maybe laws, or at least official attitudes, had changed dramatically and he believed that he and William were no longer at risk of being deemed "illegal aliens". Or, after being resident in the UK for so long, perhaps the brothers were by then deemed to be naturalised citizens. Maybe their previous army service played a part. Who knows? I tend to suspect that Jack just became heartily sick of not being able to use his own name, and decided to come clean, whatever the cost.

It should be made clear that Jack was not ashamed of his heritage. Throughout his married life, he kept on his living room wall a picture of a young Indian woman on a swing. His older grandchildren had somehow learned of Jack being married and widowed before he had met their grandmother, Mary, and, knowing of his life in India, assumed that this was a photograph of his first wife. Hence the family rumour. It was in fact the photograph of his mother that his father had taken in Chakrata. It was not shame of their heritage that haunted William and Jack throughout childhood and long into adulthood, but real concerns about the implications of it.

After joining the Royal Irish Rifles, Jack was sent again to India (where else?) to patrol the India-China border. He was finally discharged on August 22, 1918, suffering from "chronic fibrosis of the back". He worked for a while as a general labourer, before resuming his trade as a painter at Harland and Wolff Shipyard in Belfast, where he remained until his retirement.

He and Mary lived out their final years close to Lisburn. They had nine children, two of whom died in infancy. Their youngest surviving child, Andrew, was barely 12-years-old when Mary died from a heart condition on November 20, 1933. *(8)* She was aged 53 years. So Jack was left to raise the family on his own. He died of bowel cancer on February 20, 1944 at Upper Plantation on the outskirts of Lisburn. He was aged 75 years. *(9)* A late daughter-in-law of his, this author's mother, once spoke of how "no one realised he was so ill, as he never complained about it. He just took to his bed and a short while afterwards he died".

According a neighbour of the family, then only a young girl, Jack was a highly respected member of the little community at Upper Plantation. During the Second World War, in which his son, Samuel, was on active service in North Africa, he would bring a wireless on to the street each evening so the neighbours could gather round and listen to the latest war news. Another former neighbour told of how an Indian door-to-door salesman arrived one day at Upper Plantation. A man of his colour being quite a novelty at the time, a crowd of local children, including herself, followed him as he called at the houses. When he came to Jack's door, the children were astounded when the pair of them launched into a full-scale conversation "in a foreign language". Doubtless they were conversing in Urdu. It seems Jack had never forgotten his mother, or her native tongue.

William Adams
Upon being discharged from the army in 1889, William went to live with his father John at Duneight, close to Annahilt. Eliza Jane and her children joined them there after her aunt Martha died in 1891. On Martha's death certificate, "Eliza Jane Adams, her niece", is cited as being present when she died. *(10)*
According to the 1901 Ireland Census, William, Eliza Jane and her three children had continued living in the house at Duneight after John died. William is described on the census as being "Head of Family' and a "Retired Pt [ie Private] Commissariat and [army] pensioner" although the census-taker wrongly spells "commissariat". By the time of the 1911 census, they are living a few miles away at Drumbeg, with Eliza Jane's son Alfred now "Head of family". In each census, William is registered in his true surname of Adams.
On August 04, 1914 Britain declared war on Germany, signalling the start of the First World War. On October 22 of that year, William again enlisted in the British Army, joining the 3rd Battalion of the Royal Irish Rifles at Lisburn. Cautious as ever, he gave his name as "William Pope" and his next of kin as "Brother, John Henry Pope, Royal Irish Rifles, Royal Barracks, Dublin". *(11)* Jack was indeed serving in the Royal Irish Rifles, but under his true name, John Henry Adams. William's army career was again short-lived. He was discharged after little more than a month because of "health issues" (presumably this refers to the epilepsy that resulted from his being kicked by a horse in 1884). There are strong indications that William moved to Belfast sometime in the 1930s. As a consequence, the date, location, and cause of his death has proved, thus far, impossible to determine.

Eliza Jane Adams
As noted above, Eliza Jane and her three children went to live with John and William at Duneight after her aunt Martha died in 1891.
On the 1901 Ireland Census, she retained the name Sturgeon (though wrongly spelt by the census-taker as "Sturgen") and described herself

as a widow. Indicative of the unsympathetic nature of language at the time, her son Samuel was described simply as, "Imbecile". The 1911 census-taker was at least better at spelling than his counterpart of 1901, correctly listing the family surname as "Sturgeon". However, although he elaborates on Samuel's condition slightly, the language is no more sympathetic, describing the lad as "Blind and Imbecile".

Eliza Jane died of heart failure in 1917 aged 67 years (indicating that she was three years old when her mother, Eliza Jane McClean, married James Sturgeon in 1853). On her death certificate, she is registered in her proper name of Eliza Jane Adams.

When she died she was living at Magherageery, a townland in the civic parish of Blaris, which lies equidistant between Lisburn and Hillsborough. (Decades later, this author, her great-nephew, was born and raised at Magherageery, along with nine siblings.) Eliza Jane's occupation is given as "House-keeper", and her marital status as "Widow". *(12)*

For all his mental and physical problems, her son, Samuel, outlived his mother and at least one and possibly both of his brothers. He died on December 23, 1934 of tuberculosis at Downpatrick, described as, "An inmate of Down Mental Hospital. Late of Blaris, Co. Down." *(13)*

[Alfred] Henry Pope

Henry Pope died of malaria at Kandy in Ceylon in 1891. He was aged 54 years. *(14)* Although they probably kept in touch by letter, the last time John Adams and Henry Pope met in person was at Peshawar in 1873, when John was recovering from cholera. Similarly, William and Jack never met Henry again after he left Somerset for Ceylon in 1884, although one imagines they too kept in touch by letter. There can be no doubt that Henry Pope saved the lives of William and Jack. Those of us who came after them owe our existence to him.

(1 Copy of the registration of the marriage of John Henry Adams and Lillie Farrell courtesy of the Irish General Register Office, www.irishgenealogy.ie
(2 Copy of the registration of the death of Lillie Adams (nee Farrell) courtesy of the Irish General Register Office via www.irishgenealogy.ie
(3 Census returns for 1901, National Archives of Ireland, http://www.census.nationalarchives.ie/
(4 Census returns for 1911, National Archives of Ireland, http://www.census.nationalarchives.ie/
(5 Copy of the registration of the marriage of John Henry Adams and Mary McMann courtesy of Irish General Register Office, www.irishgenealogy.ie

(6 Membership details of the original Ulster Volunteer Force, the Public Records Office Northern Ireland (PRONI), https://www.nidirect.gov.uk/campaigns/public-record-office-northern-ireland-proni

(7 Jack's Attestation papers for the Royal Irish Rifles were destroyed by fire in Dublin during the 1916 Rising. However, details of his service exist in the form of an official notification of his medical discharge; British Army Service And Award Roll 1914 - 1920; and on William's Royal Irish Rifles Attestation papers, in which he cites his next of kin as: "Brother: John Henry 'Pope', Royal Irish Rifles, Royal Barracks Dublin". https://www.fold3.com

(8 Copy of death certificate courtesy of the Public Records Office Northern Ireland (PRONI), https://www.nidirect.gov.uk/campaigns/public-record-office-northern-ireland-proni

(9 Copy of death certificate courtesy of the Public Records Office Northern Ireland (PRONI), https://www.nidirect.gov.uk/campaigns/public-record-office-northern-ireland-proni

(10 Copy of the registration of the death of Martha McClean courtesy of the Irish General Register Office, www.irishgenealogy.ie

(11 British Army Attestation Papers for William Pope (Regimental No. 9419) the Royal Irish Rifles, https://www.fold3.com

(12 Copy of death certificate courtesy of the Public Records Office Northern Ireland (PRONI), https://www.nidirect.gov.uk/campaigns/public-record-office-northern-ireland-proni

(13 Copy of death certificate courtesy of the Public Records Office Northern Ireland (PRONI), https://www.nidirect.gov.uk/campaigns/public-record-office-northern-ireland-proni

(14 Listed on the British Army's "Army Returns - Deaths - 1891 to 1895", https://www.fold3.com

Printed in Great Britain
by Amazon